The Road

subterranean lives

CHRONICLES OF ALTERNATIVE AMERICA

Bradford Verter, series editor

ADVISORY BOARD
Gerald Early
Ann Fabian
Helen L. Horowitz
Regina Kunzel
David Roediger

Subterranean Lives reprints first-person accounts from the nineteenth and twentieth centuries by members of oppositional or stigmatized subcultures; memoirs by men and women who lived, whether by circumstance, inclination, or design, outside of the bounds of normative bourgeois experience. They include tramps, sexworkers, cultists, criminals, drug addicts, physically disabled people, sexual minorities, bohemians, revolutionaries, and other individuals who have survived on the margins, within the interstices, and across the boundaries of American society. Each volume presents either a book-length memoir or a selection of shorter texts in their entirety, together with an introduction and notes.

The Road, Jack London
    Todd DePastino, editor
Fitz-Hugh Ludlow, *The Hasheesh Eater: Being Passages
    from the Life of a Pythagorean,*
    Stephen Rachman, editor

The Road

Jack London

Edited and with an Introduction by

Todd DePastino

Rutgers University Press
New Brunswick, New Jersey, and London

Library of Congress Cataloging-in-Publication Data

London, Jack, 1876–1916
    The road / Jack London ; edited and with an introduction by Todd DePastino.
        p. cm. — (Subterranean lives)
        Includes bibliographical references.
        ISBN-13: 978-0-8135-3806-8 (alk. paper)
        ISBN-13: 978-0-8135-3807-5 (pbk. : alk. paper)
        1. London, Jack, 1876–1916—Travel—United States. 2. Authors, American—20th century—Biography. 3. Prisoners—United States—Biography. 4. Tramps—United States—Biography. 5. Railroad travel—United States. 6. Vagrancy—United States. I. DePastino, Todd. II. Title. III. Series.

PS3523.O46Z475 2006
813'.52—dc22

                                                2005023066

A British Cataloging-in-Publication record for this book is available from the British Library.

Book design by Karolina Harris

Manufactured in the United States of America

Contents

Acknowledgments

I would like to thank Brad Verter for his helpful comments and for suggesting a reprint of *The Road* in the first place; David Roediger for his suggestions and insights; and Melanie Halkias at Rutgers University Press for her help in preparing the manuscript and guiding it to publication. I also wish to thank Stephanie Ross for her help in editing and revising the Introduction. I am sure she too is thankful for my resisting the urge to refer to her—in the manner of Jack London—as my "Mate Woman."

Introduction

On April 6, 1894, Jack London boarded the most luxurious passenger train in the world, the Overland Limited, and departed Oakland, California, for a six-month, ten thousand-mile journey that would change his life. Jack left no record of precisely where on the train he rode that first night. The unemployed eighteen-year-old had no money, so he did not ride in one of the aptly named Palace Cars where paying passengers relaxed in all the ornate comforts of a Victorian drawing room. The gas chandeliers and reading lamps no doubt illuminated the gilded interiors of these sumptuous salons as Jack ran alongside the accelerating train looking for his chance to leap aboard.

At just the right moment—"neither the moment before nor the moment after," as he would later write about the art of train hopping—Jack either jumped up onto one of the "bumpers," or platforms, between the cars or seized hold of the iron rods that ran beneath them. If he chose to "ride the rods," he would have had to make his way into one of the cars' four-wheel trucks, positioned inches from both the whizzing wheels beside him and the gravel and ties beneath. If he chose the bumpers, he would probably have climbed next to the "deck," or roof, of the car. Then, with the train traveling fifty miles per hour, he would either have "held her down" or crawled from deck to deck until securing his place on a "blind," the prized position at the end of a baggage or mail car. The position was "blind" because there was no door leading out to it, and therefore it was relatively safe from the "shacks," or brakemen, who might try to evict the vagrant passenger from the moving train.[1]

All of these techniques belonged to a growing repertoire of road skills that Jack London would use to make his way across North America and back with hardly a dollar in his pocket. It was an outsized adventure, an exaggerated version of the unemployed migrations made by millions of boys, men, and a few women during the economic depression of the 1890s. "You can starve at home, or you can starve on the road," was a common aphorism at the time, and many, like Jack London, chose to take their chances riding the rails. In so doing, these wayfarers forged a floating subculture that was both a product of the new urban-industrial order coming into being and a challenge to it.

For Jack, the journey was born of equal parts desperation and fascination. "I went on 'The Road,'" he later wrote, "because I couldn't keep away from it; because I hadn't the price of the railroad fare in my jeans; because I was so made that I couldn't work all my life on 'one same shift'; because—well, just because it was easier to than not to."[2]

By the time he set out on his odyssey, Jack was already a seasoned rail rider, a "profesh" in hobo parlance, having served his apprenticeship with some Sacramento "road kids" two years earlier. So when he heard in the spring of 1894 that an unemployed printer named Charles T. Kelly had gathered up fifteen hundred of Oakland's jobless for a rail-riding march on Washington to demand relief, he quite reasonably quit his job as a coal shoveler and fell in with the Industrial Army of the Unemployed, as the marchers called themselves. Imbued with a sense of self-made destiny that was, in turn, fed by the storybook adventures he read so obsessively as a child, London kept his distance from the down-and-out "stiffs" of the Industrial Army and imagined himself rather as a latter-day Huck Finn lighting "out for the territory ahead of the rest." Indeed, he even kept a diary of his journey, jotting down the slang, characters, and local color he encountered along the way. Already, it seems, he was attempting to transform experience into story and to become an observer of the subterranean life in which he was also by necessity a participant.[3]

The best stories that Jack London eventually told of his hoboing days can be found in *The Road,* a collection of nine nonfiction essays written more than a dozen years after his trip of 1894. Drawing heavily on London's tramp diary as well as his memory, these stories recapture the consciousness of a teenage rebel, one who gloried in mastering his environment and surviving as an outlaw by virtue of his speed, strength, and cunning. The irreverence, freewheeling humor, "delight in life," and "zest for experience" that animate London's narrative voice are so compelling that they at times obscure the depth, complexity, and maturity of these autobiographical tall tales. After all, by the time London published *The Road* in 1907, he was far removed from his life as a road kid. By then, he was the most famous author in the world, the first modern literary celebrity, and the first writer to earn a million dollars from his work. London's disillusionment with a civilization that produces millionaires as well as tramps informs all of the stories collected here, imbuing them with a mood that is sometimes bitter, sometimes wistful, and always defiant.[4]

Like *The Adventures of Huckleberry Finn, The Road* uses the picaresque—a narrative centered on the seemingly random wanderings of a roguish hero—to achieve a critical distance from the mainstream culture. For London the writer, the road offers a vantage point from which to survey the pretensions, the hypocritical morality, the stultifying manners, and the reflexive violence of the propertied classes. Viewing the dominant culture from the bottom up and the outside in, London satirizes such ridiculous refinements as eggcups and Melba toast and exposes such official corruptions as judicial graft and police brutality. From the perspective of the boxcar, the courthouses and parlors of the respectable appear deviant and grotesque, while the hobo emerges as a self-reliant and full-blooded refugee from a despoiled social order.

This trenchant social criticism, however, followed from London's mature reflection upon his hobo experiences. For the teenage "Sailor Jack," as he was nicknamed, the road had a more immediate purpose: to deliver him from the drudgery of slum life and factory labor. In many ways, London's loving devotion to the craft of hoboing—of mooching meals and finding shelter as well as hopping trains and eluding police—provided compensation for him as an unskilled industrial worker. By the 1890s, his class indeed had suffered a drastic erosion of skill and the bargaining power that came with it, due to mechanization and the ever-increasing subdivision of labor. Uneducated and bereft of a trade (though he was at pains to emphasize his experience as a seaman, slight as it was), Jack resembled so many of his generation, condemned to a life of low-wage common labor with little hope of ever achieving economic independence.

Though Jack called himself a "work beast," his condition as a factory hand, in which he had toiled more than twelve hours a day, seven days a week, more closely resembled that of an interchangeable part in a giant machine. So while life on the road, as London dryly comments, was "not all beer and skittles," it at least offered opportunity for the creativity, autonomy, and self-directed labor that life on the shop floor denied. Savage in its satire of the middle-class work ethic, *The Road* expressed merely the common sense of a working class that was destined to replenish America's great army of hoboes year after year for decades to come.[5]

It is no wonder then that Jack London proved so popular with working-class readers, including generations of literate hoboes. But *The Road,* serialized first in *Cosmopolitan* magazine, was marketed primarily to middle-class urban dwellers who were upwardly mobile and safely ensconced in professional, managerial, and clerical careers. Their fascination with the hobo world, which London was one of the first to exploit fully, betokened white-collar workers' own dreams of escape and rebellion, dreams systematically fed by a new literary mass market. In London's hands, virile tales of the road soothed the ennui plaguing the growing army of corporate pencil pushers. At the same time, London's profesh displayed the resilience, hustle, and fluid personality that the new bureaucratically administered consumer culture would celebrate and reward.

Aware of the ironies implicit in the hobo as cultural hero, Jack London never quite resolved what the road meant for himself or for a nation that was rapidly shedding its customary sources of belonging and identity. When he returned to Oakland in the early fall of 1894, Jack made two vows that foreshadowed the contradictions of his storied career: to escape poverty by writing for the mass market and to agitate for a socialist revolution. Joining the army of pencil pushers, London harnessed the guile and grit he exhibited on the road to craft stories and a public persona that satisfied the new middle-class enchantment with all things wild and uncivilized. Almost to compensate for his individualistic striving as a "vendor of brains," as he termed it, London also embraced a vision of collective emancipation for his class, one that would restore the authentic community, unalienated labor, and integrated self that London spent his whole life pursuing. The road was part of this pursuit, and the extent to which Americans followed London down the hobo path, either as riders or as readers, gives measure of the crisis that attended the nation's rise to industrial supremacy.[6]

THE MAKING OF A PROFESH

Jack London was a child of crisis. He was born in 1876 to Flora Wellman, a single mother who had twice attempted suicide during her pregnancy with Jack. Jack's father was probably William Chaney, an itinerant astrologer who had partnered with Flora in a fortune-telling business and then abandoned her upon learning of her pregnancy. When Jack was just a few months old, Flora met and married John London, a widowed farmer and jack-of-all-trades who turned to Flora for help in raising his two daughters.

The family's start was not auspicious. Jack came into the world during the worst economic depression in history, when the noun "tramp" was used for the first time to describe the new army of penniless wayfarers searching for work. When Jack turned seven, another depression sent the family reeling and eventually prompted the bank to foreclose on his stepfather's farm. The family then packed their belongings into a potato wagon and made their way to the slums of Oakland. There, at age ten, Jack began his laboring career in earnest, delivering papers, setting bowling pins, and sweeping out saloons before turning to the local cannery, where he once endured a thirty-six hour shift. After his stepfather became disabled, the fourteen-year-old Jack took up the family breadwinning, though his wages were never enough to pay for both rent and food. By the time the third and most devastating economic depression of Jack's young life struck in 1893, delivering the nation to what many thought was the brink of revolution, the family's fortunes had deteriorated so far that for them depressions were now barely distinguishable from recoveries.

Life had not always been so hard for Jack's parents. Flora came from a prosperous merchant and manufacturer's family in Ohio, while John London was raised on a farm in Pennsylvania. Their expectations for life had been shaped by the republican ideal of broad-based property ownership. A free republic, most Americans assumed, could only exist with economically independent citizens coming together under roughly equal terms as members of the so-called producing classes. Positioned between the idle rich, who bought others' labor at bargain prices, and the unfree poor, who toiled as slaves, servants, or permanent wage laborers, the producers were imagined as guarantors of the republic. It was a "free labor" ideal, one that Abraham Lincoln praised in 1859 when he spoke of "men, with their families," who "work for themselves, on their farms, in their houses, and in their shops, taking the whole product to themselves, and asking no favors of capital on the one hand, nor of hirelings or slaves on the other."[7]

Inequalities of wealth always compromised this ideal, even in Lincoln's day, while racial and gender exclusions limited its reach to white men. The property owned by these citizen-producers, after all, included the labor of wives, children, and servants who possessed few economic or political rights. Nevertheless, this patriarchal vision of a producers' republic dominated national politics from the age of Jefferson through that of Lincoln. Indeed, many who fought in the Civil War, such as John London, believed that Lincoln's pledge to a "new birth of freedom" guaranteed the "producerist" ideal.

This ideal survived into Jack London's youth, though it no longer even approximated economic reality. By the 1870s, market expansion, capital consolidation, and large-scale production had put most small property owners out of business, destroying the fictional unity of the producing classes. Now, in direct contradiction of republican principles, most Americans worked for someone else as permanent wage laborers in a growing corporate economy. This new dependence on wages made the population vulnerable to economic downturns as never before. The new wage system also concentrated capital, and therefore economic power, into relatively few hands. Instead of a harmonious republic of producers, the nation appeared divided, as the Populist Party platform of 1892 would proclaim, into "two great classes—tramps and millionaires."[8]

It was Jack London's experiences in the tramp class that prompted him finally to shed the old republican ideals of his parents' generation. In their place arose two dueling dreams that by the turn of the twentieth century competed with each other for dominance in the American imagination. The one dream was somehow to make it into the millionaire class perhaps through a combination of pluck and luck, as prescribed by Jack's favorite childhood author, Horatio Alger Jr. The other dream, one that reshaped the American working class, was to overthrow the sham republic, the corrupt plutocracy, and replace it with a true democracy, variously imagined as anarchism, socialism, or some other noncapitalist society. Unable to choose between these two dreams, Jack London would eventually pursue both. "He was a Socialist," as one friend put it, "but he wanted to beat the Capitalist at his own game."[9]

Winning at the capitalists' game was encouraged by Flora, who bred in her son a deep discontent with his surroundings and a yearning to reclaim his family's past fortune. He must never, she told him, trust the "brunette races" who shared their working-class neighborhood but instead must rely on his own superior Anglo-Saxon blood. Jack consequently came to see himself as a racially privileged outcast among his Greek, Italian, and Chinese neighbors, an "exiled prince" in search of his kingdom. Jack's illegitimate birth compounded this obsessive quest for a lost legacy. While impoverished Americans clamored for their mythic republican patrimony, Jack sought his rightful inheritance as a descendant of "liberty-loving ancestors." Thus, Jack developed a deep ambivalence toward his class. On the one hand, he sympathized with the grievances of the urban poor and admired the vitality, rebelliousness, and comradeship so evident in laboring communities. On the other hand, he shunned the increasingly multinational and multiracial aspects of those communities and fought desperately to make his own way out of the slums.[10]

His first attempt at such self-help was through crime, one of the few avenues available for slum-dwelling entrepreneurs. When he was fifteen, Jack borrowed money to buy the *Razzle Dazzle,* a single-masted sloop that he used to steal oysters from private beds in the San Francisco Bay. He earned more in a single night's work than he could in a month at the cannery. "I was a capitalist," he later explained. "It was robbery, I grant, but it was precisely the spirit of capitalism." The spirit of capitalism in this instance was literally cut-throat. The routine violence among the fishermen, guards, and thieves with whom London did battle gave the Bay Area waterfront its reputation as the homicide capital of America. When the *Razzle Dazzle* was destroyed by fire, Jack switched sides and joined the "Fish Patrol," pursuing well-armed Greek and Chinese poachers on commission. By the time Jack happened upon a party of so-called road kids for the first time while sailing up the Sacramento River (a story he relates in "Road-Kids and Gay-Cats"), he had made so many enemies on the waterfront and had seen so many of his fellow "oyster pirates" killed that he was ready to take on a new venture.[11]

Like the oyster pirates, the homeless teenagers Jack met in Sacramento specialized in robbery, usually of bindle stiffs—laborers who traveled from job to job carrying their clothes and bedding in blanket rolls, or "bindles." They also preyed upon settled Chinese residents, as was the custom with most Anglo gangs in northern California. For a few weeks, Jack begged, stole, and hopped trains with the road kids, acquiring the skills he would use later when he returned to the road as a profesh.

Still eschewing factory labor and tiring of the petty thuggery that he felt was moving him "toward death too quickly to suit my youth and vitality," Jack signed on with a seal-hunting crew bound for the Bering Sea. For seven months, the seventeen-year-old tested his mettle aboard the *Sophia Sutherland,* a floating slaughterhouse with a twelve-man crew as tough as anyone he had encountered in the waterfront saloons of Oakland and San Francisco. The work itself was hideous. Blood and fat slathered the decks and covered the men for weeks on end as seal after seal was harpooned, hauled aboard, skinned, and thrown back to the sharks. The long summer days near the Arctic Circle meant that the slaughter hardly ever stopped. The men became killers who butchered what Jack called "pretty sea-creatures" in order to feed the elite fashion markets of New York and Paris. The crew's insensitivity to life became fully apparent when one sailor, a novice seaman like Jack, took ill and lay unattended for days. When the seaman died, crew members simply stuffed his corpse into a gunnysack weighted with coal and dropped it overboard like a skinned seal. The image of the man's body slipping beneath the ocean surface would haunt Jack the rest of his life.[12]

Alienated by the slaughter at sea and the class of men who committed it, Jack returned to Oakland in the late summer of 1893 determined to settle down and work his way into a skilled craft. His timing was terrible. Two bank panics in May and July, during which depositors withdrew their money in fear of a banking collapse, had sent the nation spiraling into another depression. Wages fell to below subsistence levels, and unemployment soared. The Bay Area and the country as a whole grew restive with strikes, protests, and dark talk of revolution.

Seemingly oblivious to the crisis, Jack resolved to secure his future by mastering cutting-edge technology. He decided to become an electrician. On a tip, perhaps, he presented himself to the superintendent of a streetcar power plant and proposed a classic American bargain. He would work harder than any employee at the plant, performing whatever menial labor was available, in exchange for practical training as an electrician. The superintendent smiled and agreed to apprentice the lad, starting him as a coal shoveler. "I was willing to work," Jack recalled years later, "and he was more than willing that I should work." The naive eighteen-year-old accepted the job, which was the most grueling he would ever endure. "I still believed in the old myths which were the heritage of the American boy when I was a boy," he explained. That myth included the old producerist ideal of working from waged apprenticeship to independent mastery.[13]

The job involved shoveling a mountain of coal into an iron wheelbarrow and then passing it to the firemen in the furnace room. Jack's workday would last for as long as it took to move the mountain, usually twelve or thirteen hours. He was to work seven days a week, with one day off a month, all for a flat rate that was less than what he had earned in the cannery. The firemen at the plant watched in silent wonder as the young coal-passer shoveled and trundled the wheelbarrow at top speed all day, without even a break for lunch. The job was so physically damaging that after a few weeks Jack almost lost use of his arms and had to keep his sprained and fractured wrists bound in leather straps. The straps would remain in place for a year afterward. His deepest pain, however, came when an indignant fireman whispered to Jack the truth about his job: Jack had been hired as a common laborer to replace two middle-aged workers at less than half their wages. The superintendent never had any intention of apprenticing the boy as an electrician.

"I thought [the superintendent] was making an electrician out of me," Jack recalled bitterly. "As a matter of fact, he was making fifty dollars per month out of me. The two men I had displaced had received forty dollars each per month; I was doing the work of both for thirty dollars per month." A sense of betrayal mixed with guilt when the fireman admonished the gullible Jack for lowering the price of labor and throwing good men out of work. When Jack learned that one of the unemployed coal-passers had committed suicide in despair over his hungry family, the teenager turned in his shovel and abandoned his boyish ideals. "The thought of work was repulsive," he explained. "I didn't care if I never settled down. Learning a trade could go hang. It was a whole lot better to royster and frolic over the world in the way I had previously done. So I headed out on the adventure-path again, starting to tramp East by beating my way on the railroads."[14]

Like so many in that age of tramps and millionaires, Jack had awakened to the hobo philosophy of life.

"HALLELUJAH, I'M A BUM"

Jack London arrived at the Oakland rail yard on April 6 expecting to find "General" Charles Kelly and his men preparing for their celebrated "petition on wheels" to Washington, D.C. He discovered instead that the police had already herded the protesters onto twenty-four boxcars and freighted them out of the city. So Jack took off after them, crossing California, Nevada, Utah, Wyoming, and Nebraska in a little under two weeks. By day, he scrounged for food and shelter with the hundreds of other East-bound hoboes he met along the way. By night, he stole rides on passenger and freight trains. When Jack and his companions finally caught up with General Kelly at Council Bluffs, Iowa, the Industrial Army had swelled to more than two thousand members. "The Army made quite an imposing array," Jack scrawled in his diary, "with flags & banners & Gen. Kelly at their head astride of a fine black horse presented by an enthusiastic Council Bluffs citizen." Most welcome was the promise of regular meals and new clothing. Jack's shoes had disintegrated, so he was now walking in his socks. His coat had been destroyed by red-hot locomotive cinders, so he now had no protection against the wind and rain. The Industrial Army's commissary interested Jack London far more than the purpose of the march itself.[15]

As London makes clear in "Two Thousand Stiffs," a memoir of his travels with General Kelly and his men, Jack was *in* the Industrial Army but not *of* it. The festivity of the march and the sympathy it garnered among midwestern residents merely made "getting by" easier for a resourceful hustler. To Jack, the "stiffs" may have been "heroes," but they were "stiffs" nonetheless, easy marks to be exploited. The attempt to transcend their down-and-out status through a protest march was noble but also futile and altogether irrelevant to a free agent such as Jack. Jack and his fellow profesh skimmed everything they could from the Industrial Army, and when the cream disappeared, they moved on. "Am going to pull out in the morning," he wrote in his diary after a month with the stiffs. "I can't stand starvation."[16]

London does not discuss the politics of the march in his memoir, allowing instead an impression of a quixotic protest that was inadequate for the challenge of the moment. From the hindsight of 1907, he was right. Only a handful of marchers ever made it to Washington, and those who did were arrested for trespassing on the Capitol lawn. The real significance of the Industrial Army movement lay in its symbolism, for the boxcars of protesters headed to Washington in the spring of 1894 represented one of the last grand expressions of the "producers' republic." Inspired by a Populist businessman from Ohio named Jacob Coxey, the movement began with the idea of petitioning Congress for a massive public works program that would guarantee "honest workingmen" a living wage. Coxey and a hundred followers were to form a "Commonweal of Christ" to deliver the petition in person after a dignified march from Coxey's hometown.

So electrifying was the prospect of a "March on Washington," however, that the movement quickly outgrew Coxey's modest plans. By April, dozens of groups across the depression-wracked nation had organized their own marches on Washington. The largest, most powerful, and most militant of these came from the West, where the unemployed banded together into a huge Industrial Army. These western contingents thought nothing of commandeering supplies, including entire freight trains, as they made their way to Washington. "A different class of beings from Coxey's followers are these western crusaders," one journalist reported. "They are stalwart young fellows, hardened by exposure and full of animal life; harder men to deal with than the meek, listless, Coxey Commonwealers." The goal of these crusaders was not simply to petition Congress for public works jobs but to challenge the "moneyed powers" that had betrayed the republic. Whereas Jacob Coxey called for "good roads" as a solution to the depression, General Kelly and other Industrial Army officers sought to overthrow the "wage system" entirely by distributing productive property, in the form of public lands, to "the great army of the unemployed."[17]

The flags and banners that festooned the mobile armies advertised the movement's republican producerist ideology, as did the Civil War veterans who were given pride of place as defenders of "free labor" ideals. Extolling their marchers as hardworking producers and dispossessed patriarchs, the movement's organizers had little use for job-shirking, adventure-seeking teenagers such as Jack London. Jack and his ilk merely confirmed the stereotypes of pundits such as economist Thorstein Veblen, who judged the marchers to be professional "idlers" seeking "a temporary means of subsistence and entertainment."[18]

Veblen's characterization was, in fact, at least half accurate. Jack London stood for a large contingent of young camp followers who had joined the Industrial Army for the meals, shoes, rides, and diversion it offered. Detached from settled communities and alienated both by wage labor and shopworn republican ideals, these freewheeling youths, with their seemingly cynical, aimless, and drifting ways, were products of an economy and culture that had dealt in false promises for too long. If the Industrial Army movement represented the last gasp of producerism, it also signified the coming of age of a new western subculture of transiency that traced its origins back to the depression of the 1870s.

After two decades of boom and bust, America's tramp army had become an institution—rather than an alarming aberration—with its own customs, values, and standards. The road had emerged through twenty years of crisis as a domain all its own standing counter to the mainstream world of home and work. So while some in the Industrial Army earnestly sought a return to their Lincolnian homesteads, others, like Jack London, embraced the hobo life as a positive freedom from the exploitations of family breadwinning. Jack and his cohorts represented the vanguard of a burgeoning counterculture of homelessness that, in its heyday, would come to be known as "hobohemia."

Someone tracing Jack London's hobo journey a few years later through rail yards, boxcars, and jail cells would probably have found scrawled somewhere lyrics to a new folk anthem that trumpeted the attitude of this alternative America. Set to the tune of the old gospel hymn "Revive Us Again," "Hallelujah, I'm a Bum" at once parodied respectable society and celebrated hoboes' liberation from it:

Oh, why don't I work
Like other men do?
How the hell can I work
When the skies are so blue?

Chorus
Hallelujah, I'm a Bum,

Hallelujah, bum again,
Hallelujah, bum a handout—
Revive me again.[19]

Although one would never know it from reading *The Road,* the counterculture that produced "Hallelujah, I'm a Bum" was itself the product of a distinct labor system that had evolved in the West. Indeed, the very term "tramping" had at one time denoted the stage in the laboring life cycle when an apprentice who had earned his "competence" in a craft was sent "tramping" from job to job. Such a "journeyman" would thereby hone his skills and save his wages until he was able to set up shop on his own. After this system had broken down, journeyman status became a permanent condition, and the word "unemployment" entered the American vernacular. Job loss became a routine problem, for most employers laid workers off seasonally, and unemployed wage earners had no property of their own to tide them over. Because most Americans walked to work, losing one's job invariably meant moving. When the economy collapsed entirely, as it did three times in the late nineteenth century, the whole country seemed to pick up and move. Those who traveled farthest in search of work tended to be single white men, "tramps," who eventually learned to make do without the luxury of "home."

The American West, rapidly building up around corporate-owned mines, farms, and timber fields, held both special appeal and special peril for tramping workers. Huge armies of labor were needed to extract minerals, harvest crops, construct railroads, and build the towns and cities that sprang up like mushrooms in the late nineteenth-century West. Wages could be high, but jobs were seasonal, so moving every few weeks or months became a way of life for western tramps. With job sites geographically dispersed, western migrants had little choice but to steal train rides, a practice they came to consider "every American's inalienable right." By the early 1890s, such flamboyant train hopping so distinguished western tramps from their eastern counterparts as to earn them a colorful new appellation: "hobo." Obscure in its origin, the term eventually came to denote any homeless man. But until 1930 or so, the honorific belonged exclusively to the most mobile, independent, and assertive members of the nation's floating army, those found on the "wageworkers' frontier" of the industrial West.[20]

In *The Road*, Jack London presents himself as the epitome of the American hobo, a profesh who could ride the rails, outwit authorities, and "batter the drag," or panhandle, better than anyone else. In doing so, London extracts and distills the subcultural elements of hobo life and leaves behind as an unsavory residue the labor upon which that subculture was based. *The Road* makes little of labor, excepting London's studied avoidance of it, and perhaps suppresses those occasions when London had to resort to wage earning in order to get by. The homeless life is, of course, work itself, and London brilliantly illuminates the labor of homelessness, what he at one point calls the "unremitting and depressing toil" of securing food and shelter. But as to the distinct social and economic conditions that produced the hobo—namely, migratory labor in the West—London says nothing. *The Road,* in effect, detaches the culture associated with these conditions and then condenses and elevates it into a rebellious lifestyle all its own, one captured in the rollicking spirit of "Hallelujah, I'm a Bum."[21]

London admires only those transients untainted by labor, the "blowed-in-the-glass" hoboes (a term derived from glassblowers' practice of blowing seals of authenticity within the glass itself) who panhandle and jump trains for sport. A true hobo, he declares in "Pictures," is one who "has learned the futility of telic endeavor, and knows the delight of drifting along with the whimsicalities of Chance." With delicious irony, he even dedicates *The Road* to the late Josiah Flynt, a popular journalist with a secret penchant for the road who nonetheless publicly condemned tramps as professional idlers. London figuratively lets Flynt out of the closet and celebrates the flaunting of convention that Flynt publicly disavowed. A decade before Sinclair Lewis coined the term "hobohemia," Jack London popularized the concept in his rendering of himself as the purest expression of the hobo philosophy.[22]

This philosophy was not merely London's invention. Conditions on the wageworkers' frontier bred values, customs, and an ethic that deviated from those of the mainstream but also derived from the grim realities of working-class life. Most important to these workers was achieving a margin of autonomy from the exploitations of wage labor. With the free labor dream of independent property ownership hopelessly out of reach, hobo laborers saw no reason to accumulate savings and instead used the money they earned as a "stake" to tide them over between jobs. Such stakes also bought the opportunity to "lay off" work altogether. "It seems that when a laborer has earned a sum which road tradition has fixed as affluence, he quits," explained one investigator of hobo life in 1915. Hoboes prized what Jack London called "the sovereign right of free contract" and used their extreme mobility to bargain for higher wages and better conditions. "Hoboes are easily picqued," explained sociologist and former hobo Nels Anderson, "and they will 'walk off' the job on the slightest pretext" in order to preserve their independence and standards.[23]

The entire subculture of the road was structured to minimize transient workers' dependence on wages and to insulate them from the power of the boss. What one observer called the "code of hobo ethics" required a high degree of comradeship and the conspicuous rejection of middle-class manners and morals. When one Chicago social worker approached a voluntarily unemployed hobo and asked why he was not taking advantage of the flush job market, the hobo replied simply, "I don't need to work." When pressed, the jobless man elaborated: "To tell the truth I really wouldn't think it was *right* to do it. I'd just be taking the work away from some poor fellow who needs it, and it wouldn't be right for a man to do that when he has plenty of money in his pocket."[24]

Hobo subculture encouraged such blatant disavowals of the middle-class work ethic while also enforcing a code of mutual aid that underwrote the hobo's ability to get by without working. "When one has money he gives it to the man who needs it," explained one hobo investigator, "and when he is broke he asks the price of a meal from the man who has it." Such reciprocity also governed life in the hobo "jungles," the campsites near railroad division points where hoboes ate, rested, and exchanged supplies and information. These "marvels of cooperation," as one observer called them, temporarily shielded migratories from the labor market and made it possible for them to travel long distances without resorting to wage earning.[25] By the early twentieth century, the hobo army had grown so large as to command a prominent share of urban space in the Midwest and West. If Jack London had hit the road ten or fifteen years later, he would have found a denser and more formal institutional network running to and from the cores of the region's cities. Such vibrant commercial districts as West Madison Street in Chicago and South of Market in San Francisco served as the "main stems" of the hobo world, offering a variety of services from cheap lodging to job placement. The main stem harbored an array of brothels, shops, saloons, theaters, gambling dens, employment agencies, and "workingmen's hotels," all catering to the hobo with a stake.

The same rules that governed life on the road also applied in the "Rialto of the hobo," where laborers marked their arrival to town "with a period of more or less riotous living." As one former hobo recalled of Minneapolis's Gateway district, "After working for a couple of months or more in a construction camp . . . they would come into town with their pockets full of money; and then there would be a prodigious celebration! Everybody was welcome to share in the 'stiff's' prosperity; and everyone did!"[26] This custom of treating others to one's prosperity, a practice ingrained in the working-class saloon culture of the period, affirmed the bonds of independent manhood through the ritualistic violation of middle-class norms.

Jack London had won his own "manhood spurs" through such rituals during his oyster pirating days. The toughest and most admired pirate in the Bay, Scratch Nelson, had bestowed upon the fifteen-year-old the privilege of drinking with him in a waterfront saloon. After six beers, paid for by Nelson, Jack left the saloon and made his way toward the *Razzle Dazzle*. Suddenly, it dawned on Jack that he had failed to reciprocate Nelson's ritual generosity. Jack had, in effect, failed an important test of working-class manhood. "I could feel myself blushing with shame," he recalled. "I have blushed many times in my life, but never have I experienced so terrible a blush as that one." After breaking down in tears, Jack returned to the saloon and virtually treated the house, throwing "overboard my old values of money," he wrote years later. "I had achieved a concept. Money no longer counted. It was comradeship that counted."[27]

The fear of humiliating oneself as a man among men, a fear that haunted Jack London throughout his life, was a common experience in an all-male world with complicated gender rules. Hoboes' class identity, their sense of themselves as wage earners, was inextricably bound with those behaviors and characteristics that they esteemed as "manly." Chief among these was avoiding the obligations not only of work but also of home. Just as the workplace represented the rule of the boss, the home represented the rule of women. Both were to be resisted. It was through his initiation into saloon life that Jack, as he later put it, "escaped from the narrowness of woman's influence into the wide free world of men." Hoboes such as Jack considered domesticity and the work ethic as two halves of a "feminized" middle-class value system that kept men in "wage slavery." Embracing the romance of the road meant rejecting "woman's influence" and middle-class family values. On Chicago's main stem, according to labor activist Elizabeth Gurley Flynn, hoboes "regarded the city workers as stay-at-home softies—'scissorbills.' They referred to the wife as 'the ball and chain.'"[28]

To resist domestication, hoboes confined their interactions with women to transient and commercial exchanges. As *The Road*'s accounts of "battering the drag" attest, women were an important source of charity for hoboes. In exchange for food, Jack London had to deny his hobohemian identity and feign an allegiance to sentimental middle-class values.

Although London makes no mention of it in *The Road,* women were also important as a source of sex, prostitution being a key attraction on the main stem. London himself championed the institution of the brothel, which he called an "intelligently ordered clearing house of the passions." His view echoed prevailing opinion within hobohemia that idealized prostitution as a way of enjoying sex without domestic entanglements. When asked by a sociologist in the 1890s whether he ever frequented prostitutes, one hobo responded matter-of-factly, "a man can't get along without that—it's God's arrangement."[29]

Homosexual relationships within hobohemia served the same function: to preserve hoboes' "manhood" by shielding them from "feminine" influences and obligations. Such relationships were common, though by no means universal, in a same-sex subculture that routinely brought men into close contact with one another. Although his description betrays no eroticism, Jack London's account in "Hoboes That Pass in the Night" of men lying "over, and under, and around one another" aboard a boxcar is suggestive of the erotic opportunities afforded by the road. Opportunity came also on the main stem, whose saloons, theaters, parks, baths, and lodging houses served an overlapping gay subculture of the city. The partnerships that men formed on the road and the main stem sometimes involved an erotic component and sometimes genuine romance. "Many of these [relationships] are not more than a few days' duration," explained Nels Anderson, "but while they last they are very intense and sentimental."[30]

Far more common than sex between hoboes of equal status were the predatory relationships between veterans of the road, called "jockers" or "wolves," and younger initiates, known as "lambs," "prushuns," or "punks." (The term "gay" itself probably evolved from the hobo slang "gay-cat," another term for a tenderfoot hobo.) Within days of hitting the road, a rail-riding teenager could expect to be besieged by wolves promising money, protection, and instruction in the art of "getting by" in exchange for a sexual relationship. Rare is the account of hobo life that does not mention the ubiquity of these wolf-punk relationships. Indeed, before it was bowdlerized in the 1920s, the road's most famous folk song, "The Big Rock Candy Mountain," originally told a sardonic tale of a punk's disenchantment with a wolf's promises of "cigarette trees" and "streams of alcohol" in a land of milk and honey. In the earliest version, the punk finally leaves his wolf, declaring:

I've hiked and hiked till my feet are sore
And I'll be damned if I hike any more
To be buggered sore like a hobo's whore
In the Big Rock Candy Mountains.

The song's author, Mac McClintock, had himself done battle with wolves during his days as a road kid. "There were times when I fought like a wildcat or ran like a deer," he recalled, "to preserve my independence and my virginity." While Jack London sanitizes his discussion of the wolf-punk relationship in "Road-Kids and Gay-Cats," making no mention of sex, he also, like McClintock, emphasizes that he never served as a punk. "I did not take kindly to possession" is all that London offers by way of explanation.[31]

As London and McClintock's language suggests, the stakes in these battles between wolf and road kid were "manly" independence and self-possession, not heterosexual identity. Like many laboring subcultures, hobohemia did not categorize its members in terms of "heterosexual" and "homosexual" but rather in terms of phallic domination and submission. Wolves were dominant because they "owned" their punks and refused to be penetrated. They were no less "manly" because they had sex with other men. Likewise, the stigma of the punk had little to do with that of homosexual desire or "queerness." Rather, punks were seen as weak or "unmanly" (they were often given girls' nicknames) and could only redeem their manhood by besting others in contests of strength and skill, such as preying on other punks. Unlike the husbands and fathers of the middle class, men on the road gained their manhood not through heterosexual desire or relations with women but only through relations with other men. "I didn't know anything about girls," London once wrote about his early problems courting women. "I had been too busy being a man."[32] In Jack London's world, only men could confer the title of "man."

The virile persona that made Jack London famous derived from this plebeian culture of manliness. London's passion for wrestling, boxing, and other manly arts as well as his legendary feats of physical courage and daring and his lifelong difficulty in understanding and relating to women were all evidence of a fragile gender identity that needed to be reconstituted time and again through public performances of masculine prowess.

His deep identification with that most predatory and pack-oriented of North American mammals, the wolf, suggests just how profoundly this gender system imprinted itself on London. Later in life, his closest friend, George Sterling, would address London in erotically charged letters as "My Darling Wolf," while London would sign "Wolf" at the bottom of his letters and insist that his lovers call him such. He titled his first book *The Son of the Wolf;* he named his mansion "Wolf House"; and he wrote his most famous novel, *The Call of the Wild,* about a dog who trades his domesticity for the primal freedoms of an Arctic wolf pack.[33]

In *The Road,* London bestows upon the wolf the title of "profesh." As he puts it in "Road-Kids and Gay-Cats," "the profesh are the aristocracy of The Road. They are the lords and masters, the aggressive men, the primordial noblemen, the *blond beasts* so beloved of Nietzsche." Such overblown language, with its labored reference to the German philosopher Friedrich Nietzsche, sounds desperate and pleading to the contemporary ear. The very strain of this passage signals the extent of the crisis that the profesh was intended to assuage, a crisis not only of gender but also of race. For London, the road liberated white men from the multiethnic and multiracial confines of the slums, allowing hoboes to rediscover the "blond beasts" within and reclaim their rightful place atop the racial hierarchy. The explicitly racist language and cartoonish portrayals of African Americans in *The Road* only reinforce London's depiction of the road as a preserve of noble white manhood.[34]

London's racial imagination had come together during the great third wave of immigration between 1880 and 1920, when masses of dispossessed peasants from southern and eastern Europe swamped urban slums and recomposed the American working class. These, along with the Chinese, Mexicans, and African Americans of northern California, constituted the "brunette races" so despised by Jack London's mother. In the Bay Area, white workers alarmed by falling wages focused their ire on the low-paid Chinese and helped win passage in 1882 of the Chinese Exclusion Act, which shut off immigration from China. Even with this victory, native-born workers of northern European extraction saw themselves as under siege and threatened with the loss of what Jack London called the sacred "heritage" of his "American ancestry."[35]

This same sense of racial grievance prevailed on the road where hoboes cultivated an identity not just as men but as *white* men in counterdistinction to the legions of nonwhite migratory laborers circulating on the wageworkers' frontier. Representatives from just about every nationality and racial group in America could be found in mining, construction, and agricultural camps all over the West. Although they often worked side by side with hoboes, foreign-born and nonwhite migrants showed little of the hobo's free-spending and freewheeling ways. These nonhoboes tended to ship out together in large gangs of common laborers, stay on the job until it ended, and send the money they earned back to their families. Avoiding the main stem, immigrants and African Americans congregated in their own segregated boardinghouse neighborhoods and found jobs through their own networks of labor contractors. Hoboes, therefore, came to see the road as a racially privileged domain where train hopping, panhandling, and cavorting on the main stem constituted free expressions of independent whiteness.

Hobohemia did not so much shape Jack London's racial and gender imagination as it expressed the forms of whiteness and manliness that young working-class men such as Jack brought to the road. In 1894, hobohemia had not yet evolved the ideologies and politics that would challenge white workers' customary racial and gender identities. In time, however, the crucible of the road would transform working-class consciousness, and hobohemia would use the grievances, disillusionments, and rebellious impulses of plebeian life to fashion a revolutionary movement all its own, one far removed from the republican producerist world of the Industrial Army. But all this would come later, long after Jack had returned home in the fall of 1894, after he had become a world-renowned writer, and after he had his own political awakening that for a time made him the most famous revolutionary in the world.

"A VENDOR OF BRAINS"

Had Jack London been born twenty years later, he might have gone down in history as America's greatest hobo poet and propagandist. If he had hit the road in 1914 instead of 1894, his attention certainly would have been captured, if not absorbed, by the Industrial Workers of the World (IWW), a high-spirited labor union that had mobilized the wageworkers' frontier for revolution. Believing in direct action, especially strikes and boycotts, Wobblies, as IWW members were called, sought to build a "new society within the shell of the old," not a producers' republic but an anarchist democracy achieved through One Big Union. Roving "job delegates" recruited hobo laborers by the thousands and won amazing on-the-job victories on their behalf, including improved wages and working conditions. A by-product of their organizing campaign was an elaborate hobo folklore propagated in numerous Wobbly newspapers, pamphlets, and songbooks. Here, hoboes appeared as swaggering, larger-than-life figures liberating the West from "wage slavery" and setting their sights on the more entrenched industries and pallid family workers of the East. To the Wobblies, undomesticated hoboes represented the "real proletarians," a vanguard of virile revolutionaries whose example would lead others to emancipation.[36]

One can easily imagine Jack London as a Wobbly troubadour: soapboxing on the main stem, enforcing the rule of the "red card" (IWW membership) on the road, penning satirical dispatches for the *Industrial Worker;* and perhaps contributing lyrics to that magnificent artifact of hobo subculture, the *Little Red Songbook.* Instead, Jack came to his revolutionary politics and literary career in reaction to the road, as antidotes to the fate that he believed awaited him if he remained on the hobo trail. The road had exposed him to revolutionary propaganda, to be sure. Socialist theory, he remarked, was a common topic of conversation among hoboes, and he once spent a sunny day in Boston discussing "Karl Marx and the German economists" with another bookish profesh. But it was the trials of the road itself—especially as he moved from what he called the "wild and woolly West," where hobo subculture thrived, to the "effete East," where "tramps" were objects of scorn—that scared Jack London into abandoning the individualistic values of his youth and the masculine code of his class.[37]

There were no trials at first, however, when Jack left the Industrial Army for Chicago, where he slept in a Salvation Army hotel and toured the grounds of the great World's Columbian Exposition. An excursion from there to his aunt's farmhouse in Michigan introduced him to his cousin, Ernest Everhard, whose name was so irresistibly Londonian that Jack would eventually use it for the protagonist of his novel, *The Iron Heel*. It was only after leaving Michigan, traveling east, that he encountered the pain, suffering, and sordidness of the "submerged tenth."[38]

Jack's eastern itinerary began in New York City and then turned to Buffalo and Niagara Falls; Harrisburg, Pennsylvania; Washington, D.C.; Baltimore; Boston; Vermont; Montreal; and Ottawa before returning him to the more hospitable hobo grounds of British Columbia, Canada. Hardship followed him everywhere. In New York City, which he found depressing and alienating, a police officer's billy club almost cracked his skull, leaving him, as he explains in "Bulls," with a lifelong aversion to law enforcement. In Buffalo, Jack was arrested on the "charge of Tramp" and sentenced to thirty days of "unprintable" and "unthinkable" horror in the Erie County Penitentiary. "My patriotic American citizenship [at the sentencing]," he writes in "Pinched," "received a shock from which it has never fully recovered." Equally shocking was the horsewhipped family he saw near Harrisburg, a scene he describes in "Pictures." Moving on to Washington, Jack found panhandling so difficult that he took a job in a livery stable in exchange for bunking with the horses. New England and eastern Canada too were inhospitable. The bulls were harsher, the residents stingier, and the tramps older and less assertive than in the hobo West.[39]

By the time he returned home in September or October, Jack London had seen enough of the "submerged tenth" to know what eventually became of sturdy, unskilled hoboes like himself. When the muscles tired and the body grew old, poor laborers all ended up in what Jack called the "Social Pit." As he later explained in an essay titled "How I Became a Socialist":

> I battered on the drag and slammed back gates with them, or
> shivered with them in box cars and city parks, listening the while to
> life-histories which began under auspices as fair as mine, with

digestions and bodies equal to and better than mine, and which ended there before my eyes in the shambles at the bottom of the Social Pit.

And as I listened my brain began to work. The woman of the streets and the man of the gutter drew very close to me. I saw the picture of the Social Pit as vividly as though it were a concrete thing, and at the bottom of the Pit I saw them, myself above them, not far, and hanging on to the slippery wall by main strength and sweat. And I confess a terror seized me. What when my strength failed? when I should be unable to work shoulder to shoulder with the strong men who were as yet babes unborn?[40]

It was through this realization, London writes, that "my rampant individualism was pretty effectively hammered out of me, and something else as effectively hammered in."[41] That something else, Jack discovered after many hours in the Oakland Public Library, was socialism. A year after his homecoming, Jack would begin delivering street-corner orations calling upon workers to rise up against their capitalist masters. Newspapers ran stories on the remarkable "Boy Socialist" of Oakland who kept his audiences in rapt attention.

Part and parcel of Jack's conversion to socialism was his resolve once again to escape the working class. Socialism had revealed to Jack the "naked simplicities" of a seemingly "complicated civilization." The rule of capital, he realized, boiled down to a single truth: "All things were commodities, all people bought and sold." Those with only their muscle to sell were destined for the Social Pit, because muscle was the cheapest of all commodities, and it was not a renewable resource. Bereft of capital, Jack was determined to find another commodity that would keep him out of the Pit and swore an oath never to depend on his muscle again. He would run away from what his class knew as "hard work" and instead leverage himself into the middle class on the strength of his intellect. "I resolved to sell no more muscle," London recalled over a decade later, "and to become a vendor of brains."[42]

Jack attacked his "brain work" as he had the mountain of coal in the power plant. He quit his carousing and entered Oakland High

School, a nineteen-year-old man among boys. To support himself and his parents, he worked as a janitor, took odd jobs, and borrowed money from a waterfront saloon keeper who, in recognition of the working-class code of manhood, charged no interest. Jack found the pace of learning far too slow, however, so he devised a shortcut: he would skip high school altogether and enter the University of California by passing its rigorous entrance exams. Jack studied for the tests in a prep school until the headmaster expelled him for fear that he would discredit the two-year program by completing it in four months. Thus, Jack learned equations, formulas, history, and literature on his own, nineteen hours a day for twelve weeks. The cramming paid off. When Jack arrived at Berkeley campus in the fall of 1896, starch-collared "college men" gawked at the student with the sunburned face, missing front teeth (lost in a waterfront brawl), soft collar open at the throat, and huge bundle of books under his arm.

Jack lasted one semester. Lack of money and patience once again forced him to improvise a fast track. This time, he resolved simply to launch his writing career uncredentialed. He had heard that magazine editors bought good words for two cents each, so Jack set about assembling thousands of words a day into essays and short stories, jokes and verse. Pawning his books and clothes to buy paper, postage, and envelopes, Jack hammered away for fifteen hours a day at an ancient typewriter that typed only in capital letters. Rejection slips piled up five feet high on a skewer next to his desk, while rent and bills went unpaid. Yet, he kept pounding the keys until blisters formed on his fingertips, burst, and then formed again. Finally, after several months and no acceptances, Jack gave up. What followed was a typical Londonian cycle of "work beast" toil (in a laundry), disgust, and escape (to the Alaskan gold rush).

While this first writing stint failed in terms of publication, it established the notoriously punishing literary regimen that would eventually yield Jack success. When he returned from his year in the Klondike, Jack once again shut himself up in his room and wrote for hours and days on end, sometimes without breaking to eat. After several weeks, his skin turned sallow from lack of sunlight. It was a masochistic approach to writing that Jack would follow for the rest of his life: sleeping five hours a night or less and writing at least one thousand polished words a day, every day. Most everything he wrote was composed in his head, drafted and proofread once, and then submitted to what he called the "editorial machine" on the other side of the continent. "I have no unfinished stories," he later told a reporter.[43] "Invariably, I complete every one I start. If it's good, I sign it and send it out. If it's not good, I sign it and send it out."[44] Jack's "antiliterary" method defied the refined, contemplative ideals that were the hallmarks of nineteenth-century genteel literature. He saw writing not only as a way of avoiding the Social Pit but also as a manly art in itself, a test of strength and endurance. Jack, in effect, applied the muscular rules of the waterfront and the road—the performance of manliness—to the vending of brains.

Jack's grueling literary endeavor was born not merely of economic necessity but also of his need to reconcile his white-collar aspirations to his code of manly conduct. In swearing never again to sell his muscle, Jack struck a Faustian bargain: he traded what he knew as his manhood for the knowledge and power of a "feminized" middle class.

It certainly did not help Jack's conflicted psyche that so many of those who smoothed the way for his new career were women. Ina Coolbrith, poet and librarian at the Oakland Public Library, was the first "cultured" person Jack ever knew, and after his return from the road, she introduced him to a new world of parlors and drawing rooms. Through her contacts, Jack met the sons and daughters of well-to-do families. Among them was Mabel Applegarth, a student at the University of California at Berkeley, who taught Jack about art, music, and literature as well as proper diction and table etiquette. Even Jack's involvement with the local Socialist Labor Party, composed largely of propertied reformers and intellectuals, derived from Jack's wish to get closer to that feminine middle-class realm where, as he put it, all was "fine and noble and gracious." By aping genteel manners and morals and by shrewdly playing up his good looks and Huck Finn persona, Jack learned how to "get by" in the middle class. He performed as expected, but instead of being rewarded with a "set down," or proper meal, as he would have on the road, he was invited to dwell on what he called the "parlor floor of society."[45]

To compensate for what his class might construe as a humiliating submission of his manhood, Jack redefined writing and the writer's life as the achievement of independent mastery, even domination. Through writing, Jack believed, he could become the profesh of the parlor world. When he turned down an editorship at *Cosmopolitan* magazine after his early success, London explained, "I want to be free to write what delights me . . . no office work for me; no routine; no doing this set task and that set task. No man over me."[46] Writing, like the road, served as an escape from the mechanized routines of factory life. But, also like the road, the literary world held perils of its own, wolves who would demand submission. "No man over me" effectively served as the motto of Jack London's career.

The successful writer, Jack eventually came to understand, dominated the reader, especially the "gentle reader"—most often figured as a young woman—that nineteenth-century editors imagined as representing their ideal audience. Jack's earliest work pandered to the domestic prejudices of such readers rather than challenged them. His early tramp stories and essays, for example, sensationalized the road as the "river of oblivion" and evoked pathos for the kids carried off by it.[47] After his Klondike experience, however, Jack's moody stories of "outdoor" hardship virtually celebrated the exotic and fearsome situations that subverted civilized codes of behavior. The atmospherics of these stories, so saturated with violence and the cruel indifference of nature, were designed, in fact, to shock, offend, and above all captivate "gentle readers."

London vividly depicts a moment of such literary "success" in *Martin Eden,* an autobiographical novel about a scar-faced laborer who rises to literary celebrity. When a young, well-heeled benefactress, modeled on Mabel Applegarth, gives the brawny Martin the genteel education that allows him to escape the slums, he returns the favor by reading from his graphic and amoral work:

"How dreadful!" she cried, when he had finished. "It is horrible— unutterably horrible!"

He noted her pale face, her eyes wide and tense, and her clenched hands, with secret satisfaction. He had succeeded. . . . No matter whether she liked it or not, it had gripped her and mastered her, made her sit there and listen and forget the details.[48]

Here, the physicality of London's composition method meets its counterpart in reader response, which London ideally imagines as physical submission to the text, even rape. By subjecting the gatekeepers of domestic culture to the harsh code and humiliations of the out-of-doors world, he exacts revenge for his own submission to their rules. The stories Jack sent off to the editorial machine after his return from the Klondike demand submission in the sense that they abandon the Victorian domestic point of view and compel readers to identify with heroes who learn the ways of the wolf in order to survive.

For once, Jack's timing was perfect. By 1899, when he broke through and sold "An Odyssey of the North" to *Atlantic Monthly,* the literary market was hungering for the kind of naturalistic themes and forceful style that would become hallmarks of London's work. The editorial establishment whose gates Jack London was later credited with crashing had, in fact, been searching for writers with his vigorous prose and masculine appeal. "We want stories," declared magazine pioneer and publishing magnate Frank Munsey, ". . . not washed-out studies of effete human nature, not weak tales of sickly sentimentality, not 'pretty' writing."[49] This turn against the conventions of sentimental and domestic fiction in the 1890s corresponded with the growth of national advertising and the emergence of new print, photograph, and papermaking technologies that transformed the publishing industry. A genteel, family-oriented business catering to high-minded readers exploded in the last decade of the nineteenth century into a modern commercial enterprise marketing to a mass audience. A new generation of publishing entrepreneurs called for stories with dramatic economy, fast-paced narratives, and unmannered prose. The goal was to stimulate and entertain readers rather than edify and uplift. By the turn of the century, newspapers, magazines, and books increasingly traded in material that explored the "underside" of society and human nature and ventured beyond the boundaries of polite "civilization."

It was indeed middle-class readers' fears of their own "overcivilization" that shaped the new literary marketplace of Jack London's era. Just as hobohemia represented a white working-class revolt against the loss of "mastery," a new cult of the "strenuous life" in the 1890s signaled a middle-class male rebellion against feminine domesticity and corporate bureaucracy. Middle-class culture had long posited women as the moral guardians of the domestic sphere, gently influencing the home's inhabitants while men battled for dominance in the marketplace. With the rise of salaried work in corporate offices, the feminine refinements of home were experienced as stifling rather than refreshing. The entrepreneurial values of competitiveness, self-reliance, and risk-taking appeared to be waning in a corporate economy and Victorian culture that encouraged passivity and conformity. Augmenting the middle-class male's "crisis of cultural authority" was the growing power of immigrant groups clustered in urban centers and the increased visibility of women in the public sphere, especially social reform and urban leisure.[50] With the 1890 census confirming that the American frontier had closed, white middle-class men scrambled for new ways to recapture their manly vigor in the urban industrial age.

Jack London's stories of "de-civilization" and mastery in the wilds met the needs of this white-collar market precisely. His own experiences on the so-called parlor floor of society had awakened him to the middle-class desire for escape, regression, and regeneration. These fantasies fueled the popularity of his Klondike stories, especially *The Call of the Wild*. London's familiarity with the dilemmas of the middle-class psyche encouraged him to revisit the road with a new perspective. He had originally experienced the hobo life as a plebeian escape from industrial discipline and wage dependency. Twelve years later, a new middle-class angle of vision sorted and recast those memories in a way that spoke to white-collar needs and desires. Ironically, *The Road* remains most true to London's working-class roots not so much in its glorifying of the profesh but in its subtle critique of that for which he stands.

REVISITING THE ROAD

Jack London wrote *The Road* at the peak of his fame, wealth, and literary power. He was already the author of several acclaimed novels—including *The Call of the Wild, The Sea Wolf,* and *White Fang*—and had just completed a speaking tour that paid an astounding six hundred dollars per week plus expenses. The opulent "Palace Cars" whose rails he had once ridden carried him home in first-class style as he dined on his favorite undercooked duck washed down with sweet German wine. He and his new wife, Charmian Kittredge, whom he called his "Mate Woman," settled back into their 130-acre "dream ranch" in the Sonoma Valley, where he had once envisioned glorious days of unalienated labor both out-of-doors and at the typewriter.

Jack had more than beaten the capitalists at their own game; he had trounced them. Why, then, was he so unhappy? "The things that I had fought and burned the midnight oil for," he later wrote, "had failed me." Success and fame were not just empty illusions; they were wolves that hounded him. The brave new publishing world that had rescued Jack from the Social Pit had also fashioned him into the first modern American celebrity, a distinctly twentieth-century commodity. His swashbuckling life and handsome face became fodder for a new gossip industry so hungry for material that Jack felt imprisoned on his dream ranch. His wealth offered little consolation. "I could sleep in only one bed at a time," Jack lamented, "and of what worth was an income of a hundred porterhouses a day when I could eat only one?"[51]

Such conspicuous disregard for money coyly sidestepped a private extravagance that kept Jack churning out fiction like a one-man assembly line. London's dream ranch became a financial sinkhole as he expanded it tenfold and added amenities for its growing population of prize horses, bulls, cows, pigs, and chickens. The horses alone cost more to feed per day than an average laborer earned per month. Hungry for cash, Jack London became the first writer to sell endorsements; his name and image appeared in advertisements for cigars, breath mints, clothing, and many other consumer products. "I have become a parasite," the still ardent Socialist confessed to a reporter.[52]

While Jack's bloated lifestyle may have made him feel like a parasite, his feverish writing taught him that brain vending was still labor. He was no longer figuratively chained to a machine as he had been in the cannery, but he now felt "handcuffed" to editors who demanded a constant supply of fresh, original stories packaged in the proven conventions of popular fiction. Desperate for material, he bought plots from other writers (including the young Sinclair Lewis) and scoured headlines for stories, a practice that invited well-publicized charges of plagiarism. He quarreled with publishers constantly over payment and played publishing houses against each other as they bid for his work. All the while he complained that editors were trying to make a "eunuch" out of him by demanding that his stories conform to "cowardly bourgeois instincts."[53]

Predictably, Jack's disgust with publishers and himself aroused his urge for escape. This time, he and Charmian conceived the most grandiose of "adventure-paths": they would build a forty-foot state-of-the-art yacht and spend the next seven years sailing around the world. "Spare no expense," he told the builder. "Let everything on the *Snark* [a name Jack borrowed from a Lewis Carroll poem] be of the best."[54] As construction costs soared (he would eventually spend an astronomical thirty thousand dollars on the vessel), Jack turned to a novel literary technique that would soon become the norm: he peddled story ideas in return for advance payment.

In particular, Jack solicited publishers to sponsor his trip around the world in exchange for exclusive rights to his travel stories. Several publishers accepted the deal. In grand Londonian style, Jack collected money from them all and poured it into the *Snark*. When one magazine then advertised that it would be covering Jack's entire journey, the others discovered that the rights they had purchased were hardly exclusive. *Cosmopolitan* wrote Jack in December 1906 asking for him to return the magazine's advance of two thousand dollar. In an uncharacteristically formal letter containing some hard-nosed accounting (and no mention of his prior agreement to christen his boat *Cosmopolitan Magazine*), Jack explained to the editors that he was "not prepared at the present moment" to return the money. Then, he offered a deal. If *Cosmopolitan* would be willing to pay him fifteen cents a word, he would write a "series of tramp reminiscences" in as many words as necessary to repay the debt. If the editors liked the series, he could extend it. *Cosmopolitan* agreed to the terms, and within two weeks he submitted "Confession" and "Holding Her Down." When the magazine decided to continue the series, Jack dashed off seven more stories over the next two months.[55]

The improvised terms of publication made it difficult for Jack to conceive his road stories in anything but anecdotal form. *Cosmopolitan* ran the articles in the order Jack sent them, and the Macmillan Company did the same when it published the collection as a book in November 1907. Rather than a full-length narrative with well-developed plot, themes, and characters, *The Road* proceeds haphazardly, jumping back and forth in time and digressing often before returning to the ideas that open his essays. This lack of unity and extended treatment has made *The Road* one of Jack London's least reprinted and critically examined books. Most readers have judged it as mere rollicking entertainment. Even his daughter, Joan London, claimed that in *The Road,* "Jack escaped happily into the past, reliving his adventures" in order to relieve the pressures of the present.[56]

Such dismissive judgments ignore the heated controversy that greeted Jack's road stories when they appeared. Most reviewers criticized the book for its morals rather than its literary quality, charging a lack of "wholesomeness" in the way it "glorified the morally disintegrating influence of tramp life."[57] George Brett, Jack's own editor at Macmillan, as well as his friend George Sterling expressed alarm that Jack would even consider risking his endorsements and book sales by writing about his disreputable tramp days. Such objections remind us both that the hobo was not yet the folksy character he would later become and that in choosing the hobo as a literary subject, London deliberately crossed the boundary of middle-class respectability.

By crossing this boundary, of course, London played to the ongoing cultural revolt against feminine domesticity. One must imagine *The Road* as titillating middle-class readers as it pulls aside the curtain on a fearsome and inscrutable tramp world. In letting his readers in on this subculture, London gives them a powerful new perspective from which to critique their own sheltered lives. The book's generous use of subcultural slang, which London translates clearly within the text, also provides readers with a new insider language, a portion of which would eventually filter into the mainstream. (It is fascinating to consider which words remain in everyday use—such as "punk," "bum," "ditch," "nerve," and "handout"—and which do not.) More than merely a nostalgic series of adventures stories, *The Road* takes a controversial stand in a middle-class culture at war with itself.

The book is more complicated still, for its defiant celebration of the road as a release from bourgeois respectability contains an undertone of self-criticism. In rebelling against Victorian manners, Jack-the-profesh replicates the hustle, deceptions, exploitations, and injustices of the capitalist marketplace. London's unapologetic descriptions of his embezzling in Kelly's Army should not be read as a sign of his moral indifference. Rather, his matter-of-fact attitude suggests merely how routine such crimes are in American society. Indeed, in London's book, the road itself is but a microcosm of a larger social world whose grasping brutality leads some to mastery and others to the Social Pit. The profesh, from this perspective, is not to be admired; he is to be resisted. In his lectures, London had forcefully denounced the "parasites on the backs of labor" that kept ten million Americans in crushing poverty.[58] The profesh, London implies, is merely another parasitic by-product of capitalism.

London makes his analogy to capitalism explicit in "The Pen" when he compares his role as a prison trusty, or "hall-man," to that of his "brother bandits" in capitalist society. Hall-men such as London ruled by fear and kept inmates hungry in order to skim profits and keep the population under control. "We but patterned ourselves after our betters outside the walls," London coolly explains, "who, on a larger scale, and under the respectable disguise of merchants, bankers, and captains of industry, did precisely what we were doing." London momentarily abandons his detachment when speaking of the "unprintable horrors" committed by hall-men. "I say 'unprintable'; and in justice I must also say 'unthinkable,'" he adds.[59] Though he claims only to have observed such horrors, which included rape, assault, and perhaps homicide, London lets slip that all hall-men were required to participate in the manhandling of inmates. As a privileged hall-man, London no doubt left the penitentiary with blood on his hands.

The Road extends this self-criticism into a less sanguinary realm by drawing an analogy between the profesh on the road and the writer in the literary marketplace. Presumably like readers immersed in his book, London was drawn to the road by the "new vernacular" he heard there. "With every word they uttered," he writes in "Road-Kids and Gay-Cats," "the lure of The Road laid hold of me more imperiously."[60] Language, London makes clear, is also key to "getting by" on the road, for the successful beggar must spin yarns that "hit home" with his "mark." He even cynically maintains that hoboing served as an "apprenticeship" for his literary career by teaching him that "art is only consummate artfulness." In the most remarkable passage in the book, Jack London comes clean (the passage is from the aptly titled essay "Confession") with an elaborate analogy that equates his audience with "victims" of a confidence game:

> For know that upon his ability to tell a good story depends the success of the beggar. First of all, and on the instant, the beggar must "size up" his victim. After that, he must tell a story that will appeal to the peculiar personality and temperament of that particular victim. . . . The successful hobo must be an artist. He must create spontaneously and instantaneously—and not upon a theme selected from the plentitude of his own imagination, but upon the theme he reads in the face of the person who opens the door. . . . At the back door, out of inexorable necessity, is developed the convincingness and sincerity laid down by all authorities on the art of the short-story. Also, I quite believe it was my tramp-apprenticeship that made a realist out of me. Realism constitutes the only goods one can exchange at the kitchen door for grub.[61]

London's nonchalance belies a cynicism made all the more startling given London's famous commitment to "SINCERITY" (often spelled out in capitals) as the most important quality in literature. Here, sincerity is but a ruse. London implies that his stories derive not from the integrity of his imagination but rather from a base calculation of the market. This admission renders both the profesh and the wolfish writer as something less than a Nietzschean "blond beast." For all his success, London admits, he had never gotten beyond brain vending.

This alienation had been long in the making. London's career had thrived on the stark contrasts he drew between wolf and punk, domination and submission, masculine and feminine, savagery and civilization, proletarian and bourgeois. Now, unable either to abide in the wolfish half of these dichotomies or transcend them altogether, London found himself adrift, once again an "exiled prince" in search of a kingdom. He inched in his thinking toward androgyny, especially in light of his "Mate Woman" Charmian, but the comradeship and fellowship he craved remained elusive.

As he had once explained to Charmian, "I went into the world early, and I adventured among many different classes. A newcomer in any class, I naturally was reticent concerning my real self, which such a class could not understand, while I was superficially locquacious in order to make my entry into such a class popular and successful. And so it went, from class to class, from clique to clique. No intimacies, a continuous hardening, a superficial loquacity so clever, and an inner reticence so secret, that the one was taken for the real, the other never dreamed of."[62] Having invested so heavily in his various public personas in order to "get by," London failed to develop an integrated self. As a result, he lacked the sense of belonging and identification with others that had been the object of his quest all along.

After he had submitted his road stories to *Cosmopolitan* and set sail on the leaking *Snark,* Jack took to the stateroom and began work on a novel that would document his estrangement from both his working-class roots and his comfortable bourgeois life. The book's first title was *Success,* later changed to *Martin Eden,* and it told the story of Jack's rise to fortune in the literary marketplace. Martin, the novel's hero, pursues writing to escape poverty, eschewing the aesthetic ideals of Art and Beauty. When Martin at last achieves success, he finds himself alienated from his literary labor and yet unable to embrace art for its own sake. On a ship sailing for the South Pacific, Martin is at home among neither the "bestial creatures" in the sailors' forecastle nor the "good and kindly" passengers of the staterooms. Gripped by despair and seeing no way out, Martin lowers himself into the ocean and sinks to the bottom. It is only in death that Martin Eden recovers his original wholeness: "And at the instant he knew, he ceased to know."[63]

Martin Eden's bleak vision, along with Jack's well-known alcoholism and morphine addiction, fueled speculation that London's own death in 1916 at age forty was deliberately self-inflicted (most scholars identify the cause as kidney failure hastened by drug use). The most intriguing questions raised by Jack London's premature death, however, involve the roads he did not live long enough to take. What might have happened had he survived into the 1930s, when the greatest of all economic depressions sent millions to the road? Might he have escaped his disillusionment by embracing the white male fantasies of fascism? Or, might his fervor for revolutionary belonging have led him to the Communist Party and its accompanying social movements?

By then, he certainly would have found legions of other politically engaged, working-class writers forging a new proletarian literature, of which he himself was considered the most important precursor. This "proletarian avant-garde," in turn, launched many writers and artists on London's path from the slums to celebrity.[64] This path became a veritable rut as American mass culture matured into a hegemonic global power by midcentury. As the first great success story of this new cultural system, London would remain an icon of the American Dream's dark side, the embodiment of the peculiar hazards and burdens that mass culture celebrity so often entails. It was not until another poor boy genius, Elvis Presley, recapitulated London's dizzying ascent and subsequent self-destruction that our culture possessed as vivid and compelling an example of the American failure of success.

As for *The Road,* it too left a divided legacy, overshadowed by the more acclaimed successors it had, in part, inspired. In positing the hobo as a heroic refugee from American civilization, Jack London played upon and complicated a key trope, or figure of speech, in American literature, the Whitmanesque open road. D. H. Lawrence called it "the exultant message of American Democracy, of souls in the Open Road, full of glad recognition, full of fierce readiness, full of the joy of worship, when one soul see a greater soul."[65] London's depiction of a damaged soul on the road blazed a trail followed by the likes of John Dos Passos (*The 42nd Parallel*), Woody Guthrie (*Bound for Glory*), Jack Kerouac (*On the Road*), and numerous others. All of these works, in their own ways, suggest how the perennial American romance of the road eventually runs up against its limits, either in restless striving or homeless despair. As with Jack London, the great American drifter loses this romance when confronted by the reality of the streets, where excitement turns into hustle, escape into alienation, and freedom into homelessness. If Jack London had lived to see the Great Depression, he might have once again lit out for the territories, only this time in search of home rather than adventure.

NOTES

1. Jack London, "Rods and Gunnels," in *Jack London on the Road: The Tramp Diary and Other Hobo Writings,* ed. Richard W. Etulain (Logan: Utah State University Press, 1979), 91.

2. Jack London, "Road-Kids and Gay-Cats," in *The Road,* presented in this volume.

3. Mark Twain, *The Adventures of Huckleberry Finn* (New York: Tom Doherty, 1985), 294.

4. Jack London, "Confession," in *The Road.*

5. Jack London, "John Barleycorn," in *Novels and Social Writings,* ed. Donald Pizer (New York: Library of America, 1982), 1038; London, "Bulls," in *The Road.*

6. Jack London, "What Life Means to Me," in *The Portable Jack London,* ed. Earle Labor (New York: Penguin, 1994), 478.

7. Abraham Lincoln, "Annual Address before the Wisconsin State Agricultural Society, at Milwaukee, Wisconsin, September 30, 1859," in *Abraham Lincoln: Speeches and Writings* (New York: Library of America, 1989), 97.

8. "Populist Party Platform, July 4, 1892," in *Documents in American His-*

tory, vol. 1, ed. Henry Steele Commager (New York: Appleton, Century, Crofts, 1963), 593.

9. Alex Kershaw, *Jack London: A Life* (New York: St. Martin's, 1997), 96.

10. Richard O'Connor, *Jack London: A Biography* (Boston: Little, Brown, 1964), 35; Joan D. Hedrick, *Solitary Comrade: Jack London and His Work* (Chapel Hill: University of North Carolina Press, 1982), xvi; London, "Bulls," in *The Road.*

11. London, "What Life Means to Me," in *The Portable Jack London,* 476.

12. London, "John Barleycorn," in *Novels and Social Writings,* 1008; Jack London, *The Sea Wolf* (New York: Heritage Press, 1961 [1904]), 153.

13. London, "What Life Means to Me," in *The Portable Jack London,* 477; London, "John Barleycorn," in *Novels and Social Writings,* 1032.

14. London, "John Barleycorn," in *Novels and Social Writings,* 1035, 1038.

15. London, "Tramp Diary," in *Jack London on the Road,* 41.

16. Ibid., 54.

17. Shirley Plumer Austin, "The Downfall of Coxeyism," *Chautauquan* 19 (July 1894): 452; Henry Vincent, *The Story of the Commonweal* (New York: Arno, 1969 [1894]), 154–55.

18. T. B. Veblen, "The Army of the Commonweal," *Journal of Political Economy* 2 (June 1894): 457.

19. George Milburn, *The Hobo's Hornbook: A Repertory for a Gutter Jongleur* (New York: Ives Washburn, 1930), 97.

20. James J. Davis, *The Iron Puddler: My Life in the Rolling Mills and What Became of It* (Indianapolis: Bobbs-Merrill, 1922), 11.

21. London, "Holding Her Down," in *The Road.*

22. London, "Pictures," in *The Road.*

23. Carleton H. Parker, *The Casual Laborer and Other Essays* (New York: Harcourt, Brace, and Howe, 1920), 78; London, "John Barleycorn," in *Novels and Social Writings,* 1032; Nels Anderson, *The Hobo: The Sociology of the Homeless Man* (Chicago: Phoenix Books, 1965 [1923]), 74.

24. Frederick Mills, quoted in Gregory R. Woirol, *In the Floating Army: F. C. Mills on Itinerant Life in California, 1914* (Urbana: University of Illinois Press, 1992), 79; Alice Willard Solenberger, *One Thousand Homeless Men: A Study of Original Records* (New York: Russell Sage Foundation, 1911), 143–44.

25. Powers Hapgood, Journal, Vol. 2, October 16, 1920, Box 2, Powers Hapgood Papers (St. Paul: Minnesota Historical Society); Harry Kemp, "The Lure of the Tramp," *Independent* 70 (June 8, 1991): 1270.

26. Charles Ashleigh, *Rambling Kid* (London: Faber, 1930), 92.

27. London, "John Barleycorn," in *Novels and Social Writings,* 975, 977, 978, 981.

28. Ibid., 937; Elizabeth Gurley Flynn, *Rebel Girl* (New York: International Publishers, 1973), 103.

29. Kershaw, *Jack London,* 105; Roger Bruns, *Knights of the Road: A Hobo History* (New York: Metheun, 1980), 141.

30. London, "Hoboes That Pass in the Night," in *The Road*; Nels Anderson, "The Juvenile and the Tramp," *Journal of Criminology and Criminal Law* 14 (August 1922): 306.

31. Mac McClintock, Lyrics, "Big Rock Candy Mountain," http://www.sciencedaily.com/encyclopedia/big_rock_candy_mountain (accessed April 20, 2005); John Greenway, *American Folksongs of Protest* (Philadelphia: University of Pennsylvania Press, 1953), 201; London, "Road-Kids and Gay-Cats," in *The Road.*

32. London, "John Barleycorn," in *Novels and Social Writings,* 1023.

33. Quoted in Kershaw, *Jack London,* 105.

34. London, "Road-Kids and Gay-Cats," in *The Road.*

35. London, "'Pinched,'" in *The Road.*

36. Walker C. Smith, "The Floater as Iconoclast," *Industrial Worker,* June 4, 1910.

37. London, "Jack London in Boston," in *Jack London on the Road,* 85; London, "Two Thousand Stiffs," in *The Road.*

38. Jack London, "How I Became a Socialist," in *The Portable Jack London,* 460.

39. London, "Pen," in *The Road*; London, "'Pinched,'" in *The Road.*

40. London, "How I Became a Socialist," in *The Portable Jack London,* 460–61.

41. Ibid., 461.

42. London, "What Life Means to Me," in *The Portable Jack London,* 478.

43. London, "Martin Eden," in *Novels and Social Writings,* 663.

44. Pete Hamill, "Jack London and John Barleycorn," in Jack London, *John Barleycorn* (New York: Modern Library, 2001).

45. London, "What Life Means to Me," in *The Portable Jack London,* 478.

46. Christopher P. Wilson, *The Labor of Words: Literary Professionalism in the Progressive Era* (Athens: University of Georgia Press, 1985), 97.

47. London, "The Road," in *Jack London on the Road,* 69.

48. London, "Martin Eden," in *Novels and Social Writings,* 668.

49. Quoted in Wilson, *The Labor of Words,* 58.

50. T. J. Jackson Lears, *No Place of Grace: Antimodernism and the Transformation of American Culture, 1880–1920* (New York: Pantheon, 1981), 5.

51. London, "John Barleycorn," in *Novels and Social Writings,* 1065–66.

52. Kershaw, *Jack London,* 161.

53. Quoted in Kershaw, *Jack London,* 175; quoted in Wilson, *The Labor of Words,* 107.

54. Quoted in Kershaw, *Jack London,* 173.

55. Quoted in King Hendricks, "Introduction," in Jack London, *The Road,* ed. King Hendricks (Santa Barbara: Peregrine, 1970), xiv.

56. Quoted in Richard W. Etulain, "Introduction," in *Jack London on the Road,* 19.

57. Hendricks, "Introduction," in *The Road,* xv.

58. Quoted in Kershaw, *Jack London,* 161.

59. London, "Pen," in *The Road.*

60. London, "Road-Kids and Gay-Cats," in *The Road.*

61. London, "Confession," in *The Road.*

62. Quoted from Hedrick, *Solitary Comrade,* 44.

63. London, "Martin Eden," in *Novels and Social Writings,* 926, 927, 931.

64. Michael Denning, *The Cultural Front: The Laboring of American Culture in the Twentieth Century* (New York: Verso, 1997), 64.

65. D. H. Lawrence, *Studies in Classical American Literature* (New York: Viking, 1961 [1923]), 177.

Selected Bibliography

Anderson, Nels. *The Hobo: The Sociology of the Homeless Man*. Chicago: Phoenix Books, 1965 [1923].

Auerbach, Johnathan. *Male Call: Becoming Jack London*. Durham, NC: Duke University Press, 1996.

Cassuto, Leonard, and Jeanne Campbell Reesman, eds. *Rereading Jack London*. Stanford, Calif.: Stanford University Press, 1996.

DePastino, Todd, *Citizen Hobo: How a Century of Homelessness Shaped America*. Chicago: University of Chicago Press, 2003.

Foner, Philip. *Jack London: American Rebel*. New York: Citadel Press, 1947.

Hedrick, Joan D. *Solitary Comrade: Jack London and His Work*. Chapel Hill: University of North Carolina Press, 1982.

Higbie, Frank Tobias. *Indispensable Outcasts: Hoe Workers and Community in the American Midwest, 1880–1920*. Urbana: University of Illinois Press, 2003.

Kershaw, Alex. *Jack London: A Life*. New York: St. Martin's, 1997.

Kusmer, Kenneth L. *Down and Out, On the Road: The Homeless in American History*. New York: Oxford University Press, 2002.

Labor, Earle, ed. *The Portable Jack London*. New York: Penguin, 1994.

Labor, Earle, and Jeanne Campbell Reesman. *Jack London*. Revised ed. New York: Twayne, 1994.

London, Jack. *Jack London on the Road: The Tramp Diary and Other Hobo Writings*. Ed. Richard W. Etulain. Logan: Utah State University Press, 1979.

McClintock, James I. *White Logic: Jack London's Short Stories*. Grand Rapids, MI: Wolf House, 1975.

Stasz, Clarice. *American Dreamers: Charmian and Jack London*. New York: St. Martin's, 1988.

———. *Jack London's Women*. Amherst: University of Massachusetts Press, 2001.

Wilson, Christopher P. *The Labor of Words: Literary Professionalism in the Progressive Era*. Athens: University of Georgia Press, 1985.

A Note on the Text

This edition of *The Road* reprints the original manuscript and illustrations published by Macmillan in November 1907 rather than the articles that ran in *Cosmopolitan* magazine in 1907–1908. In tailoring London's stories to fit the magazine's readership and page size, *Cosmopolitan*'s editors cut, rephrased, and otherwise altered numerous passages in London's original typescripts. Macmillan's editors, on the other hand, adhered to the original typescripts and therefore published the stories as London conceived them.

The Road

The tall negro and I had the place of honor

The Road

by Jack London

Author of "The Call of the Wild,"

"White Fang," etc.

Illustrated

New York
The Macmillan Company
1907
All rights reserved

Copyright, 1907,
By International Magazine Company.
Copyright, 1907,
By The Macmillan Company.
Set up and electrotyped. Published November, 1907.
Norwood Press
J. S. Cushing Co.—Berwick & Smith Co.
Norwood, Mass., U.S.A.

"Speakin' in general, I 'ave tried 'em all,
The 'appy roads that take you o'er the world.
Speakin' in general, I 'ave found them good
For such as cannot use one bed too long,
But must get 'ence, the same as I 'ave done,
An' go observin' matters till they die."

—*Sestina of the Tramp-Royal.*[1]

To

Josiah Flynt

The Real Thing, Blowed in the Glass[1]

CONTENTS

ILLUSTRATIONS

The Road

CONFESSION

There is a woman in the state of Nevada to whom I once lied continuously, consistently, and shamelessly, for the matter of a couple of hours. I don't want to apologize to her. Far be it from me. But I do want to explain. Unfortunately, I do not know her name, much less her present address. If her eyes should chance upon these lines, I hope she will write to me.

It was in Reno, Nevada, in the summer of 1892. Also, it was fair-time, and the town was filled with petty crooks and tin-horns, to say nothing of a vast and hungry horde of hoboes. It was the hungry hoboes that made the town a "hungry" town. They "battered" the back doors of the homes of the citizens until the back doors became unresponsive.

A hard town for "scoffings," was what the hoboes called it at that time. I know that I missed many a meal, in spite of the fact that I could "throw my feet" with the next one when it came to "slamming a gate" for a "poke-out" or a "set-down," or hitting for a "light piece" on the street. Why, I was so hard put in that town, one day, that I gave the porter the slip and invaded the private car of some itinerant millionnaire. The train started as I made the platform, and I headed for the aforesaid millionnaire with the porter one jump behind and reaching for me. It was a dead heat, for I reached the millionnaire at the same instant that the porter reached me. I had no time for formalities. "Gimme a quarter to eat on," I blurted out. And as I live, that millionnaire dipped into his pocket and gave me . . . just . . . precisely . . . a quarter. It is my conviction that he was so flabbergasted that he obeyed automatically, and it has been a matter of keen regret ever since, on my part, that I didn't ask him for a dollar. I know that I'd have got it. I swung off the platform of that private car with the porter manoeuvring to kick me in the face. He missed me. One is at a terrible disadvantage when trying to swing off the lowest step of a car and not break his neck on the right of way, with, at the same time, an irate Ethiopian on the platform above trying to land him in the face with a number eleven. But I got the quarter! I got it!

But to return to the woman to whom I so shamelessly lied. It was in the evening of my last day in Reno. I had been out to the race-track watching the ponies run, and had missed my dinner (*i.e.* the midday meal). I was hungry, and, furthermore, a committee of public safety had just been organized to rid the town of just such hungry mortals as I. Already a lot of my brother hoboes had been gathered in by John Law, and I could hear the sunny valleys of California calling to me over the cold crests of the Sierras.[1] Two acts remained for me to perform before I shook the dust of Reno from my feet. One was to catch the blind baggage on the westbound overland that night.[2] The other was first to get something to eat. Even youth will hesitate at an all-night ride, on an empty stomach, outside a train that is tearing the atmosphere through the snow-sheds, tunnels, and eternal snows of heaven-aspiring mountains.

But that something to eat was a hard proposition. I was "turned down" at a dozen houses. Sometimes I received insulting remarks and was informed of the barred domicile that should be mine if I had my just deserts. The worst of it was that such assertions were only too true. That was why I was pulling west that night. John Law was abroad in the town, seeking eagerly for the hungry and homeless, for by such was his barred domicile tenanted.

At other houses the doors were slammed in my face, cutting short my politely and humbly couched request for something to eat. At one house they did not open the door. I stood on the porch and knocked, and they looked out at me through the window. They even held one sturdy little boy aloft so that he could see over the shoulders of his elders the tramp who wasn't going to get anything to eat at their house.

It began to look as if I should be compelled to go to the very poor for my food. The very poor constitute the last sure recourse of the

The doors were slammed in my face.

hungry tramp. The very poor can always be depended upon. They never turn away the hungry. Time and again, all over the United States, have I been refused food by the big house on the hill; and always have I received food from the little shack down by the creek or marsh, with its broken windows stuffed with rags and its tired-faced mother broken with labor. Oh, you charity-mongers! Go to the poor and learn, for the poor alone are the charitable. They neither give nor withhold from their excess. They have no excess. They give, and they withhold never, from what they need for themselves, and very often from what they cruelly need for themselves. A bone to the dog is not charity. Charity is the bone shared with the dog when you are just as hungry as the dog.

There was one house in particular where I was turned down that evening. The porch windows opened on the dining room, and through them I saw a man eating pie—a big meat-pie. I stood in the

A bone to the dog is not charity.

open door, and while he talked with me, he went on eating. He was prosperous, and out of his prosperity had been bred resentment against his less fortunate brothers.

He cut short my request for something to eat, snapping out, "I don't believe you want to work."

Now this was irrelevant. I hadn't said anything about work. The topic of conversation I had introduced was "food." In fact, I didn't want to work. I wanted to take the westbound overland that night.

"You wouldn't work if you had a chance," he bullied.

I glanced at his meek-faced wife, and knew that but for the presence of this Cerberus I'd have a whack at that meat-pie myself.[3] But Cerberus sopped himself in the pie, and I saw that I must placate him if I were to get a share of it. So I sighed to myself and accepted his work-morality.

"Of course I want work," I bluffed.

"Don't believe it," he snorted.

"Try me," I answered, warming to the bluff.

"All right," he said. "Come to the corner of blank and blank streets"—(I have forgotten the address)—"to-morrow morning. You know where that burned building is, and I'll put you to work tossing bricks."

I stood in the open door.

"All right, sir; I'll be there."

He grunted and went on eating. I waited. After a couple of minutes he looked up with an I-thought-you-were-gone expression on his face, and demanded:—

"Well?"

"I . . . I am waiting for something to eat," I said gently.

"I knew you wouldn't work!" he roared.

He was right, of course; but his conclusion must have been reached by mind-reading, for his logic wouldn't bear it out. But the beggar at the door must be humble, so I accepted his logic as I had accepted his morality.

"You see, I am now hungry," I said still gently. "To-morrow morning I shall be hungrier. Think how hungry I shall be when I have tossed bricks all day without anything to eat. Now if you will give me something to eat, I'll be in great shape for those bricks."

He gravely considered my plea, at the same time going on eating, while his wife nearly trembled into propitiatory speech, but refrained.

"I'll tell you what I'll do," he said between mouthfuls. "You come to work to-morrow, and in the middle of the day I'll advance you enough for your dinner. That will show whether you are in earnest or not."

"In the meantime—" I began; but he interrupted.

"If I gave you something to eat now, I'd never see you again. Oh, I know your kind. Look at me. I owe no man. I have never descended so low as to ask any one for food. I have always earned my food. The trouble with you is that you are idle and dissolute. I can see it in your face. I have worked and been honest. I have made myself what I am. And you can do the same, if you work and are honest."

"Like you?" I queried.

Alas, no ray of humor had ever penetrated the sombre work-sodden soul of that man.

"Yes, like me," he answered.

"All of us?" I queried.

"Yes, all of you," he answered, conviction vibrating in his voice.

"But if we all became like you," I said, "allow me to point out that there'd be nobody to toss bricks for you."

I swear there was a flicker of a smile in his wife's eye. As for him, he was aghast—but whether at the awful possibility of a reformed humanity that would not enable him to get anybody to toss bricks for him, or at my impudence, I shall never know.

"I'll not waste words on you," he roared. "Get out of here, you ungrateful whelp!"

I scraped my feet to advertise my intention of going, and queried:—

"And I don't get anything to eat?"

He arose suddenly to his feet. He was a large man. I was a stranger in a strange land, and John Law was looking for me. I went away hurriedly. "But why ungrateful?" I asked myself as I slammed his gate. "What in the dickens did he give me to be ungrateful about?" I looked back. I could still see him through the window. He had returned to his pie.

By this time I had lost heart. I passed many houses by without venturing up to them. All houses looked alike, and none looked "good." After walking half a dozen blocks I shook off my despondency and gathered my "nerve." This begging for food was all a game, and if I didn't like the cards, I could always call for a new deal. I made up my mind to tackle the next house. I approached it in the deepening twilight, going around to the kitchen door.

I knocked softly at the kitchen door.

I knocked softly, and when I saw the kind face of the middle-aged woman who answered, as by inspiration came to me the "story" I was to tell. For know that upon his ability to tell a good story depends the success of the beggar. First of all, and on the instant, the beggar must "size up" his victim. After that, he must tell a story that will appeal to the peculiar personality and temperament of that particular victim. And right here arises the great difficulty: in the instant that he is sizing up the victim he must begin his story. Not a minute is allowed for preparation. As in a lightning flash he must divine the nature of the victim and conceive a tale that will hit home. The successful hobo must be an artist. He must create spontaneously and instantaneously—and not upon a theme selected from the plenitude of his own imagination, but upon the theme he reads in the face of the person who opens the door, be it man, woman, or child, sweet or crabbed, generous or miserly, good-natured or cantankerous, Jew or Gentile, black or white, race-prejudiced or brotherly, provincial or universal, or whatever else it may be. I have often thought that to this training of my tramp days is due much of my success as a story-writer. In order to get the food whereby I lived, I was compelled to tell tales that rang true. At the back door, out of inexorable necessity, is developed the convincingness and sincerity laid down by all authorities on the art of the short-story. Also, I quite believe it was my tramp-apprenticeship that made a realist out of me. Realism constitutes the only goods one can exchange at the kitchen door for grub.

After all, art is only consummate artfulness, and artfulness saves many a "story." I remember lying in a police station at Winnipeg, Manitoba. I was bound west over the Canadian Pacific. Of course, the police wanted my story, and I gave it to them—on the spur of the moment. They were landlubbers, in the heart of the continent, and what better story for them than a sea story? They could never trip me up on that. And so I told a tearful tale of my life on the hell-ship *Glenmore*. (I had once seen the *Glenmore* lying at anchor in San Francisco Bay.)

I was an English apprentice, I said. And they said that I didn't talk like an English boy. It was up to me to create on the instant. I had been born and reared in the United States. On the death of my parents, I had been sent to England to my grandparents. It was they who had apprenticed me on the *Glenmore*. I hope the captain of the *Glenmore* will forgive me, for I gave him a character that night in the Winnipeg police station. Such cruelty! Such brutality! Such diabolical ingenuity of torture! It explained why I had deserted the *Glenmore* at Montreal.

But why was I in the middle of Canada going west, when my grandparents lived in England? Promptly I created a married sister who lived in California. She would take care of me. I developed at length her loving nature. But they were not done with me, those hard-hearted policemen. I had joined the *Glenmore* in England; in the two years that had elapsed before my desertion at Montreal, what had the *Glenmore* done and where had she been? And thereat I took those landlubbers around the world with me. Buffeted by pounding seas and stung with flying spray, they fought a typhoon with me off the coast of Japan. They loaded and unloaded cargo with me in all the ports of the Seven Seas. I took them to India, and Rangoon, and China, and had them hammer ice with me around the Horn and at last come to moorings at Montreal.[4]

And then they said to wait a moment, and one policeman went forth into the night while I warmed myself at the stove, all the while racking my brains for the trap they were going to spring on me.

I groaned to myself when I saw him come in the door at the heels of the policeman. No gypsy prank had thrust those tiny hoops of gold through the ears; no prairie winds had beaten that skin into wrinkled leather; nor had snow-drift and mountain-slope put in his walk that reminiscent roll. And in those eyes, when they looked at me, I saw the unmistakable sun-wash of the sea. Here was a theme, alas! with half a dozen policemen to watch me read—I who had never sailed the China seas, nor been around the Horn, nor looked with my eyes upon India and Rangoon.

I was desperate. Disaster stalked before me incarnate in the form of that gold-ear-ringed, weather-beaten son of the sea. Who was he? What was he? I must solve him ere he solved me. I must take a new orientation, or else those wicked policemen would orientate me to a cell, a police court, and more cells. If he questioned me first, before I knew how much he knew, I was lost.

But did I betray my desperate plight to those lynx-eyed guardians of the public welfare of Winnipeg? Not I. I met that aged sailorman glad-eyed and beaming, with all the simulated relief at deliverance that a drowning man would display on finding a life-preserver in his last despairing clutch. Here was a man who understood and who would verify my true story to the faces of those sleuth-hounds who did not understand, or, at least, such was what I endeavored to play-act. I seized upon him; I volleyed him with questions about himself. Before my judges I would prove the character of my savior before he saved me.

He was a kindly sailorman—an "easy mark." The policemen grew impatient while I questioned him. At last one of them told me to shut up. I shut up; but while I remained shut up, I was busy creating, busy sketching the scenario of the next act. I had learned enough to go on with. He was a Frenchman. He had sailed always on French merchant vessels, with the one exception of a voyage on a "lime-juicer." And last of all—blessed fact!—he had not been on the sea for twenty years.

The policeman urged him on to examine me.

"You called in at Rangoon?" he queried.

I nodded. "We put our third mate ashore there. Fever."

If he had asked me what kind of fever, I should have answered, "Enteric," though for the life of me I didn't know what enteric was. But he didn't ask me. Instead, his next question was:—

"And how is Rangoon?"

"All right. It rained a whole lot when we were there."

"Did you get shore-leave?"

"Sure," I answered. "Three of us apprentices went ashore together."

"Do you remember the temple?"

"Which temple?" I parried.

"The big one, at the top of the stairway."

If I remembered that temple, I knew I'd have to describe it. The gulf yawned for me.

I shook my head.

"You can see it from all over the harbor," he informed me. "You don't need shore-leave to see that temple."

I never loathed a temple so in my life. But I fixed that particular temple at Rangoon.

"You can't see it from the harbor," I contradicted.

"You can't see it from the town. You can't see it from the top of the stairway. Because—" I paused for the effect. "Because there isn't any temple there."

"But I saw it with my own eyes!" he cried.

"That was in—?" I queried.

"Seventy-one."

"It was destroyed in the great earthquake of 1887," I explained. "It was very old."

There was a pause. He was busy reconstructing in his old eyes the youthful vision of that fair temple by the sea.

"The stairway is still there," I aided him. "You can see it from all over the harbor. And you remember that little island on the right-hand side coming into the harbor?" I guess there must have been one there (I was prepared to shift it over to the left-hand side), for he nodded. "Gone," I said. "Seven fathoms of water there now."

I had gained a moment for breath. While he pondered on time's changes, I prepared the finishing touches of my story.

"You remember the custom-house at Bombay?"

He remembered it.

"Burned to the ground," I announced.

"Do you remember Jim Wan?" he came back at me.

"Dead," I said; but who the devil Jim Wan was I hadn't the slightest idea.

I was on thin ice again.

"Do you remember Billy Harper, at Shanghai?" I queried back at him quickly.

That aged sailorman worked hard to recollect, but the Billy Harper of my imagination was beyond his faded memory.

"Of course you remember Billy Harper," I insisted. "Everybody knows him. He's been there forty years. Well, he's still there, that's all."

And then the miracle happened. The sailorman remembered Billy Harper. Perhaps there was a Billy Harper, and perhaps he had been in Shanghai for forty years and was still there; but it was news to me.

For fully half an hour longer, the sailorman and I talked on in similar fashion. In the end he told the policemen that I was what I represented myself to be, and after a night's lodging and a breakfast I was released to wander on westward to my married sister in San Francisco.

But to return to the woman in Reno who opened her door to me in the deepening twilight. At the first glimpse of her kindly face I took my cue. I became a sweet, innocent, unfortunate lad. I couldn't speak. I opened my mouth and closed it again. Never in my life before had I asked any one for food. My embarrassment was painful, extreme. I was ashamed. I, who looked upon begging as a delightful whimsicality, thumbed myself over into a true son of Mrs. Grundy, burdened with all her bourgeois morality.[5] Only the harsh pangs of the belly-need could compel me to do so degraded and ignoble a thing as beg for food. And into my face I strove to throw all the wan wistfulness of famished and ingenuous youth unused to mendicancy.

"You are hungry, my poor boy," she said.

I had made her speak first.

I nodded my head and gulped.

"It is the first time I have ever . . . asked," I faltered.

"Come right in." The door swung open. "We have already finished eating, but the fire is burning and I can get something up for you."

She looked at me closely when she got me into the light.

"I wish my boy were as healthy and strong as you," she said. "But he is not strong. He sometimes falls down. He just fell down this afternoon and hurt himself badly, the poor dear."

She mothered him with her voice, with an ineffable tenderness in it that I yearned to appropriate. I glanced at him. He sat across the table, slender and pale, his head swathed in bandages. He did not move, but his eyes, bright in the lamplight, were fixed upon me in a steady and wondering stare.

"Just like my poor father," I said. "He had the falling sickness. Some kind of vertigo. It puzzled the doctors. They never could make out what was the matter with him."

She looked at me closely when she got me
into the light.

"He is dead?" she queried gently, setting before me half a dozen
soft-boiled eggs.

"Dead," I gulped. "Two weeks ago. I was with him when it happened. We were crossing the street together. He fell right down. He was never conscious again. They carried him into a drug-store. He died there."

And thereat I developed the pitiful tale of my father—how, after my mother's death, he and I had gone to San Francisco from the ranch; how his pension (he was an old soldier), and the little other money he had, was not enough; and how he had tried book-canvassing. Also, I narrated my own woes during the few days after his death that I had spent alone and forlorn on the streets of San Francisco. While that good woman warmed up biscuits, fried bacon, and cooked more eggs, and while I kept pace with her in taking care of all that she placed before me, I enlarged the picture of that poor orphan boy and filled in the details. I became that poor boy. I believed in him as I believed in the beautiful eggs I was devouring. I could have wept for myself. I know the tears did get into my voice at times. It was very effective.

In fact, with every touch I added to the picture, that kind soul gave me something also. She made up a lunch for me to carry away. She put in many boiled eggs, pepper and salt, and other things, and a big apple. She provided me with three pairs of thick red woollen socks. She gave me clean handkerchiefs and other things which I have since forgotten. And all the time she cooked more and more and I ate more and more. I gorged like a savage; but then it was a far cry across the Sierras on a blind baggage, and I knew not when nor where I should find my next meal. And all the while, like a death's-head at the feast, silent and motionless, her own unfortunate boy sat and stared at me across the table. I suppose I represented to him mystery, and romance, and adventure—all that was denied the feeble flicker of life that was in him. And yet I could not forbear, once or twice, from wondering if he saw through me down to the bottom of my mendacious heart.

"But where are you going to?" she asked me.

"Salt Lake City," said I. "I have a sister there—a married sister." (I debated if I should make a Mormon out of her, and decided against it.) "Her husband is a plumber—a contracting plumber."

Now I knew that contracting plumbers were usually credited with making lots of money. But I had spoken. It was up to me to qualify.

"They would have sent me the money for my fare if I had asked for it," I explained, "but they have had sickness and business troubles. His partner cheated him. And so I wouldn't write for the money. I knew I could make my way there somehow. I let them think I had enough to get me to Salt Lake City. She is lovely, and so kind. She was always kind to me. I guess I'll go into the shop and learn the trade. She has two daughters. They are younger than I. One is only a baby."

Of all my married sisters that I have distributed among the cities of the United States, that Salt Lake sister is my favorite. She is quite real, too. When I tell about her, I can see her, and her two little girls, and her plumber husband. She is a large, motherly woman, just verging on beneficent stoutness—the kind, you know, that always cooks nice things and that never gets angry. She is a brunette. Her husband is a quiet, easy-going fellow. Sometimes I almost know him quite well. And who knows but some day I may meet him? If that aged sailorman could remember Billy Harper, I see no reason why I should not some day meet the husband of my sister who lives in Salt Lake City.

On the other hand, I have a feeling of certitude within me that I shall never meet in the flesh my many parents and grandparents—you see, I invariably killed them off. Heart disease was my favorite way of getting rid of my mother, though on occasion I did away with her by means of consumption, pneumonia, and typhoid fever. It is true, as the Winnipeg policemen will attest, that I have grandparents living in England; but that was a long time ago and it is a fair assumption that they are dead by now. At any rate, they have never written to me.

I hope that woman in Reno will read these lines and forgive me my gracelessness and unveracity. I do not apologize, for I am unashamed. It was youth, delight in life, zest for experience, that brought me to her door. It did me good. It taught me the intrinsic kindliness of human nature. I hope it did her good. Anyway, she may get a good laugh out of it now that she learns the real inwardness of the situation.

To her my story was "true." She believed in me and all my family, and she was filled with solicitude for the dangerous journey I must make ere I won to Salt Lake City. This solicitude nearly brought me to grief. Just as I was leaving, my arms full of lunch and my pockets bulging with fat woollen socks, she bethought herself of a nephew, or uncle, or relative of some sort, who was in the railway mail service, and who, moreover, would come through that night on the very train on which I was going to steal my ride. The very thing! She would take me down to the depot, tell him my story, and get him to hide me in the mail car. Thus, without danger or hardship, I would be carried straight through to Ogden. Salt Lake City was only a few miles farther on. My heart sank. She grew excited as she developed the plan and with my sinking heart I had to feign unbounded gladness and enthusiasm at this solution of my difficulties.

Just as I was leaving, with my arms full of lunch.

Solution! Why I was bound west that night, and here was I being trapped into going east. It *was* a trap, and I hadn't the heart to tell her that it was all a miserable lie. And while I made believe that I was delighted, I was busy cudgelling my brains for some way to escape. But there was no way. She would see me into the mail-car—she said so herself—and then that mail-clerk relative of hers would carry me to Ogden. And then I would have to beat my way back over all those hundreds of miles of desert.

But luck was with me that night. Just about the time she was getting ready to put on her bonnet and accompany me, she discovered that she had made a mistake. Her mail-clerk relative was not scheduled to come through that night. His run had been changed. He would not come through until two nights afterward. I was saved, for of course my boundless youth would never permit me to wait those two days. I optimistically assured her that I'd get to Salt Lake City quicker if I started immediately, and I departed with her blessings and best wishes ringing in my ears.

But those woollen socks were great. I know. I wore a pair of them that night on the blind baggage of the overland, and that overland went west.

Barring accidents, a good hobo, with youth and agility, can hold a train down despite all the efforts of the train-crew to "ditch" him—given, of course, night-time as an essential condition. When such a hobo, under such conditions, makes up his mind that he is going to hold her down, either he does hold her down, or chance trips him up. There is no legitimate way, short of murder, whereby the train-crew can ditch him. That train-crews have not stopped short of murder is a current belief in the tramp world. Not having had that particular experience in my tramp days I cannot vouch for it personally.

On the Rods.

But this I have heard of the "bad" roads. When a tramp has "gone underneath," on the rods, and the train is in motion, there is apparently no way of dislodging him until the train stops. The tramp, snugly ensconced inside the truck, with the four wheels and all the framework around him has the "cinch" on the crew—or so he thinks, until some day he rides the rods on a bad road. A bad road is usually one on which a short time previously one or several trainmen have been killed by tramps. Heaven pity the tramp who is caught "underneath" on such a road—for caught he is, though the train be going sixty miles an hour.

The "shack" (brakeman) takes a coupling-pin and a length of bell-cord to the platform in front of the truck in which the tramp is riding. The shack fastens the coupling-pin to the bell-cord, drops the former down between the platforms, and pays out the latter. The coupling-pin strikes the ties between the rails, rebounds against the bottom of the car, and again strikes the ties. The shack plays it back and forth, now to this side, now to the other, lets it out a bit and hauls it in a bit, giving his weapon opportunity for every variety of impact and rebound. Every blow of that flying coupling-pin is freighted with death, and at sixty miles an hour it beats a veritable tattoo of death. The next day the remains of that tramp are gathered up along the right of way, and a line in the local paper mentions the unknown man, undoubtedly a tramp, assumably drunk, who had probably fallen asleep on the track.

As a characteristic illustration of how a capable hobo can hold her down, I am minded to give the following experience. I was in Ottawa, bound west over the Canadian Pacific. Three thousand miles of that road stretched before me; it was the fall of the year, and I had to cross Manitoba and the Rocky Mountains. I could expect "crimpy" weather, and every moment of delay increased the frigid hardships of the journey. Furthermore, I was disgusted. The distance between Montreal and Ottawa is one hundred and twenty miles. I ought to know, for I had just come over it and it had taken me six days. By mistake I had missed the main line and come over a small "jerk" with only two locals a day on it.[1] And during these six days I had lived on dry crusts, and not enough of them, begged from the French peasants.

Furthermore, my disgust had been heightened by the one day I had spent in Ottawa trying to get an outfit of clothing for my long journey. Let me put it on record right here that Ottawa, with one exception, is the hardest town in the United States and Canada to beg clothes in; the one exception is Washington, D.C. The latter fair city is the limit. I spent two weeks there trying to beg a pair of shoes, and then had to go on to Jersey City before I got them.

But to return to Ottawa. At eight sharp in the morning I started out after clothes. I worked energetically all day. I swear I walked forty miles. I interviewed the housewives of a thousand homes. I did not even knock off work for dinner. And at six in the afternoon, after ten hours of unremitting and depressing toil, I was still shy one shirt, while the pair of trousers I had managed to acquire was tight and, moreover, was showing all the signs of an early disintegration.

At six I quit work and headed for the railroad yards, expecting to pick up something to eat on the way. But my hard luck was still with me. I was refused food at house after house. Then I got a "hand-out." My spirits soared, for it was the largest hand-out I had ever seen in a long and varied experience. It was a parcel wrapped in newspapers and as big as a mature suit-case. I hurried to a vacant lot and opened it. First, I saw cake, then more cake, all kinds and makes of cake, and then some. It was all cake. No bread and butter with thick firm slices of meat between—nothing but cake; and I who of all things abhorred cake most! In another age and clime they sat down by the waters of Babylon and wept. And in a vacant lot in Canada's proud capital, I, too, sat down and wept . . . over a mountain of cake. As one looks upon the face of his dead son, so looked I upon that multitudinous pastry. I suppose I was an ungrateful tramp, for I refused to partake of the bounteousness of the house that had had a party the night before. Evidently the guests hadn't liked cake either.

That cake marked the crisis in my fortunes. Than it nothing could be worse; therefore things must begin to mend. And they did. At the very next house I was given a "set-down." Now a "set-down"

It was the largest hand-out I ever saw.

Evidently the guests hadn't liked cake either.

is the height of bliss. One is taken inside, very often is given a chance to wash, and is then "set-down" at a table. Tramps love to throw their legs under a table. The house was large and comfortable, in the midst of spacious grounds and fine trees, and sat well back from the street. They had just finished eating, and I was taken right into the dining room—in itself a most unusual happening, for the tramp who is lucky enough to win a set-down usually receives it in the kitchen. A grizzled and gracious Englishman, his matronly wife, and a beautiful young Frenchwoman talked with me while I ate.

A "Set-down."

I wonder if that beautiful young Frenchwoman would remember, at this late day, the laugh I gave her when I uttered the barbaric phrase, "two-bits."[2] You see, I was trying delicately to hit them for a "light piece." That was how the sum of money came to be mentioned.

"What?" she said. "Two-bits," said I. Her mouth was twitching as she again said, "What?" "Two-bits," said I. Whereat she burst into laughter. "Won't you repeat it?" she said, when she had regained control of herself. "Two-bits," said I. And once more she rippled into uncontrollable silvery laughter. "I beg your pardon," said she; "but what . . . what was it you said?" "Two-bits," said I; "is there anything wrong about it?" "Not that I know of," she gurgled between gasps; "but what does it mean?" I explained, but I do not remember now whether or not I got that two-bits out of her; but I have often wondered since as to which of us was the provincial.

When I arrived at the depot, I found, much to my disgust, a bunch of at least twenty tramps that were waiting to ride out the blind baggages of the overland. Now two or three tramps on the blind baggage are all right. They are inconspicuous. But a score! That meant trouble. No train-crew would ever let all of us ride.

I may as well explain here what a blind baggage is. Some mail-cars are built without doors in the ends; hence, such a car is "blind." The mail-cars that possess end doors, have those doors always locked. Suppose, after the train has started, that a tramp gets on to the platform of one of these blind cars. There is no door, or the door is locked. No conductor or brakeman can get to him to collect fare or throw him off. It is clear that the tramp is safe until the next time the train stops. Then he must get off, run ahead in the darkness, and when the train pulls by, jump on to the blind again. But there are ways and ways, as you shall see.

When the train pulled out, those twenty tramps swarmed upon the three blinds. Some climbed on before the train had run a car-length. They were awkward dubs, and I saw their speedy finish. Of course, the train-crew was "on," and at the first stop the trouble began. I jumped off and ran forward along the track. I noticed that I was accompanied by a number of the tramps. They evidently knew their business. When one is beating an overland, he must always keep well ahead of the train at the stops. I ran ahead, and as I ran, one by one those that accompanied me dropped out. This dropping out was the measure of their skill and nerve in boarding a train.

For this is the way it works. When the train starts, the shack rides out the blind. There is no way for him to get back into the train proper except by jumping off the blind and catching a platform where the car-ends are not "blind." When the train is going as fast as the shack cares to risk, he therefore jumps off the blind, lets several cars go by, and gets on to the train. So it is up to the tramp to run so far ahead that before the blind is opposite him the shack will have already vacated it.

I dropped the last tramp by about fifty feet, and waited. The train started. I saw the lantern of the shack on the first blind. He was riding her out. And I saw the dubs stand forlornly by the track as the blind went by. They made no attempt to get on. They were beaten by their own inefficiency at the very start. After them, in the line-up, came the tramps that knew a little something about the game. They let the first blind, occupied by the shack, go by, and jumped on the second and third blinds. Of course, the shack jumped off the first and on to the second as it went by, and scrambled around there, throwing off the men who had boarded it. But the point is that I was so far ahead that when the first blind came opposite me, the shack had already left it and was tangled up with the tramps on the second blind. A half dozen of the more skilful tramps, who had run far enough ahead, made the first blind, too.

At the next stop, as we ran forward along the track, I counted but fifteen of us. Five had been ditched. The weeding-out process had begun nobly, and it continued station by station. Now we were fourteen, now twelve, now eleven, now nine, now eight. It reminded me of the ten little niggers of the nursery rhyme.[3] I was resolved that I should be the last little nigger of all. And why not? Was I not blessed with strength, agility, and youth? (I was eighteen, and in perfect condition.) And didn't I have my "nerve" with me? And furthermore, was I not a tramp-royal? Were not these other tramps mere dubs and "gay-cats" and amateurs alongside of me?[4] If I weren't the last little nigger, I might as well quit the game and get a job on an alfalfa farm somewhere.

By the time our number had been reduced to four, the whole train-crew had become interested. From then on it was a contest of skill and wits, with the odds in favor of the crew. One by one the three other survivors turned up missing, until I alone remained. My, but I was proud of myself! No Croesus was ever prouder of his first million.[5] I was holding her down in spite of two brakemen, a conductor, a fireman, and an engineer.

And here are a few samples of the way I held her down. Out ahead, in the darkness,—so far ahead that the shack riding out the blind must perforce get off before it reaches me,—I get on. Very well. I am good for another station. When that station is reached, I dart ahead again to repeat the manoeuvre. The train pulls out. I watch her coming. There is no light of a lantern on the blind. Has the crew abandoned the fight? I do not know. One never knows, and one must be prepared every moment for anything. As the first blind comes opposite me, and I run to leap aboard, I strain my eyes to see if the shack is on the platform. For all I know he may be there, with his lantern doused, and even as I spring upon the steps that lantern may smash down upon my head. I ought to know. I have been hit by lanterns two or three times.

I have been hit by lanterns two or three times.

But no, the first blind is empty. The train is gathering speed. I am safe for another station. But am I? I feel the train slacken speed. On the instant I am alert. A manoeuvre is being executed against me, and I do not know what it is. I try to watch on both sides at once, not forgetting to keep track of the tender in front of me. From any one, or all, of these three directions, I may be assailed.

Ah, there it comes. The shack has ridden out the engine. My first warning is when his feet strike the steps of the right-hand side of the blind. Like a flash I am off the blind to the left and running ahead past the engine. I lose myself in the darkness. The situation is where it has been ever since the train left Ottawa. I am ahead, and the train must come past me if it is to proceed on its journey. I have as good a chance as ever for boarding her.

I watch carefully. I see a lantern come forward to the engine, and I do not see it go back from the engine. It must therefore be still on the engine, and it is a fair assumption that attached to the handle of that lantern is a shack. That shack was lazy, or else he would have put out his lantern instead of trying to shield it as he came forward. The train pulls out. The first blind is empty, and I gain it. As before the train slackens, the shack from the engine boards the blind from one side, and I go off the other side and run forward.

As I wait in the darkness I am conscious of a big thrill of pride. The overland has stopped twice for me—for me, a poor hobo on the bum. I alone have twice stopped the overland with its many passengers and coaches, its government mail, and its two thousand steam horses straining in the engine. And I weigh only one hundred and sixty pounds, and I haven't a five-cent piece in my pocket!

Again I see the lantern come forward to the engine. But this time it comes conspicuously. A bit too conspicuously to suit me, and I wonder what is up. At any rate I have something else to be afraid of than the shack on the engine. The train pulls by. Just in time, before I make my spring, I see the dark form of a shack, without a lantern, on the first blind. I let it go by, and prepare to board the second blind. But the shack on the first blind has jumped off and is at my heels. Also, I have a fleeting glimpse of the lantern of the shack who rode out the engine. He has jumped off, and now both shacks are on the ground on the same side with me. The next moment the second blind comes by and I am aboard it. But I do not linger. I have figured out my countermove. As I dash across the platform I hear the impact of the shack's feet against the steps as he boards. I jump off the other side and run forward with the train. My plan is to run forward and get on the first blind. It is nip and tuck, for the train is gathering speed. Also, the shack is behind me and running after me. I guess I am the better sprinter, for I make the first blind. I stand on the steps and watch my pursuer. He is only about ten feet back and running hard; but now the train has approximated his own speed, and, relative to me, he is standing still. I encourage him, hold out my hand to him; but he explodes in a mighty oath, gives up and makes the train several cars back.

The train is speeding along, and I am still chuckling to myself, when, without warning, a spray of water strikes me. The fireman is playing the hose on me from the engine. I step forward from the car-platform to the rear of the tender, where I am sheltered under the overhang. The water flies harmlessly over my head. My fingers itch to climb up on the tender and lam that fireman with a chunk of coal; but I know if I do that, I'll be massacred by him and the engineer, and I refrain.

At the next stop I am off and ahead in the darkness. This time, when the train pulls out, both shacks are on the first blind. I divine their game. They have blocked the repetition of my previous play. I cannot again take the second blind, cross over, and run forward to the first. As soon as the first blind passes and I do not get on, they swing off, one on each side of the train. I board the second blind, and as I do so I know that a moment later, simultaneously, those two shacks will arrive on both sides of me. It is like a trap. Both ways are blocked. Yet there is another way out, and that way is up.

So I do not wait for my pursuers to arrive. I climb upon the upright ironwork of the platform and stand upon the wheel of the hand-brake. This has taken up the moment of grace and I hear the shacks strike the steps on either side. I don't stop to look. I raise my arms overhead until my hands rest against the down-curving ends of the roofs of the two cars. One hand, of course, is on the curved roof of one car, the other hand on the curved roof of the other car. By this time both shacks are coming up the steps. I know it, though I am too busy to see them. All this is happening in the space of only several seconds. I make a spring with my legs and "muscle" myself up with my arms. As I draw up my legs, both shacks reach for me and clutch empty air. I know this, for I look down and see them. Also I hear them swear.

I make a spring with my legs and "muscle" myself up with my arms.

I look down and see them.

I am now in a precarious position, riding the ends of the down-curving roofs of two cars at the same time. With a quick, tense movement, I transfer both legs to the curve of one roof and both hands to the curve of the other roof. Then, gripping the edge of that curving roof, I climb over the curve to the level roof above, where I sit down to catch my breath, holding on the while to a ventilator that projects above the surface. I am on top of the train—on the "decks," as the tramps call it, and this process I have described is by them called "decking her." And let me say right here that only a young and vigorous tramp is able to deck a passenger train, and also, that the young and vigorous tramp must have his nerve with him as well.

The train goes on gathering speed, and I know I am safe until the next stop—but only until the next stop. If I remain on the roof after the train stops, I know those shacks will fusillade me with rocks. A healthy shack can "dewdrop" a pretty heavy chunk of stone on top of a car—say anywhere from five to twenty pounds. On the other hand, the chances are large that at the next stop the shacks will be waiting for me to descend at the place I climbed up. It is up to me to climb down at some other platform.

Registering a fervent hope that there are no tunnels in the next half mile, I rise to my feet and walk down the train half a dozen cars. And let me say that one must leave timidity behind him on such a *passear*. The roofs of passenger coaches are not made for midnight promenades. And if any one thinks they are, let me advise him to try it. Just let him walk along the roof of a jolting, lurching car, with nothing to hold on to but the black and empty air, and when he comes to the down-curving end of the roof, all wet and slippery with dew, let him accelerate his speed so as to step across to the next roof, down-curving and wet and slippery. Believe me, he will learn whether his heart is weak or his head is giddy.

As the train slows down for a stop, half a dozen platforms from where I had decked her I come down. No one is on the platform. When the train comes to a standstill, I slip off to the ground. Ahead, and between me and the engine, are two moving lanterns. The shacks are looking for me on the roofs of the cars. I note that the car beside which I am standing is a "four-wheeler"—by which is meant that it

I rise to my feet and walk down the train
half a dozen cars.

has only four wheels to each truck. (When you go underneath on the
rods, be sure to avoid the "six-wheelers,"—they lead to disasters.)

I duck under the train and make for the rods, and I can tell you I
am mighty glad that the train is standing still. It is the first time I
have ever gone underneath on the Canadian Pacific, and the internal
arrangements are new to me. I try to crawl over the top of the truck,
between the truck and the bottom of the car. But the space is not
large enough for me to squeeze through. This is new to me. Down
in the United States I am accustomed to going underneath on rapidly moving trains, seizing a gunnel and swinging my feet under to
the brake-beam, and from there crawling over the top of the truck
and down inside the truck to a seat on the cross-rod.

Feeling with my hands in the darkness, I learn that there is room
between the brake-beam and the ground. It is a tight squeeze. I have

to lie flat and worm my way through. Once inside the truck, I take my seat on the rod and wonder what the shacks are thinking has become of me. The train gets under way. They have given me up at last.

But have they? At the very next stop, I see a lantern thrust under the next truck to mine at the other end of the car. They are searching the rods for me. I must make my get-away pretty lively. I crawl on my stomach under the brake-beam. They see me and run for me, but I crawl on hands and knees across the rail on the opposite side and gain my feet. Then away I go for the head of the train. I run past the engine and hide in the sheltering darkness. It is the same old situation. I am ahead of the train, and the train must go past me.

I crawl on hands and knees across the rail on the opposite side and gain my feet.

The train pulls out. There is a lantern on the first blind. I lie low, and see the peering shack go by. But there is also a lantern on the second blind. That shack spots me and calls to the shack who has gone past on the first blind. Both jump off. Never mind, I'll take the third blind and deck her. But heavens, there is a lantern on the third blind, too. It is the conductor. I let it go by. At any rate I have now the full train-crew in front of me. I turn and run back in the opposite direction to what the train is going. I look over my shoulder. All three lanterns are on the ground and wobbling along in pursuit. I sprint. Half the train has gone by, and it is going quite fast, when I spring aboard. I know that the two shacks and the conductor will arrive like ravening wolves in about two seconds. I spring upon the wheel of the handbrake, get my hands on the curved ends of the roofs, and muscle myself up to the decks; while my disappointed pursuers, clustering on the platform beneath like dogs that have treed a cat, howl curses up at me and say unsocial things about my ancestors.

But what does that matter? It is five to one, including the engineer and fireman, and the majesty of the law and the might of a great corporation are behind them, and I am beating them out. I am too far down the train, and I run ahead over the roofs of the coaches until I am over the fifth or sixth platform from the engine. I peer down cautiously. A shack is on that platform. That he has caught sight of me, I know from the way he makes a swift sneak inside the car; and I know, also, that he is waiting inside the door, all ready to pounce out on me when I climb down. But I make believe that I don't know, and I remain there to encourage him in his error. I do not see him, yet I know that he opens the door once and peeps up to assure himself that I am still there.

The train slows down for a station. I dangle my legs down in a tentative way. The train stops. My legs are still dangling. I hear the door unlatch softly. He is all ready for me. Suddenly I spring up and run forward over the roof. This is right over his head, where he lurks inside the door. The train is standing still; the night is quiet, and I take care to make plenty of noise on the metal roof with my feet. I don't know, but my assumption is that he is now running forward to catch me as I descend at the next platform. But I don't descend there. Halfway along the roof of the coach, I turn, retrace my way softly, and quickly to the platform both the shack and I have just abandoned. The coast is clear. I descend to the ground on the off-side of the train and hide in the darkness. Not a soul has seen me.

I go over to the fence, at the edge of the right of way, and watch. Ah, ha! What's that? I see a lantern on top of the train, moving along from front to rear. They think I haven't come down, and they are searching the roofs for me. And better than that—on the ground on each side of the train, moving abreast with the lantern on top, are two other lanterns. It is a rabbit-drive, and I am the rabbit. When the shack on top flushes me, the ones on each side will nab me. I roll a cigarette and watch the procession go by. Once past me, I am safe to proceed to the front of the train. She pulls out, and I make the front blind without opposition. But before she is fully under way and just as I am lighting my cigarette, I am aware that the fireman has climbed over the coal to the back of the tender and is looking down at me. I am filled with apprehension. From his position he can mash me to a jelly with lumps of coal. Instead of which he addresses me, and I note with relief the admiration in his voice.

"You son-of-a-gun," is what he says.

It is a high compliment, and I thrill as a schoolboy thrills on receiving a reward of merit.

"Say," I call up to him, "don't you play the hose on me any more."

"All right," he answers, and goes back to his work.

I have made friends with the engine, but the shacks are still looking for me. At the next stop, the shacks ride out all three blinds, and as before, I let them go by and deck in the middle of the train. The crew is on its mettle by now, and the train stops. The shacks are going to ditch me or know the reason why. Three times the mighty overland stops for me at that station, and each time I elude the shacks and make the decks. But it is hopeless, for they have finally come to an understanding of the situation. I have taught them that they cannot guard the train from me. They must do something else.

And they do it. When the train stops that last time, they take after me hot-footed. Ah, I see their game. They are trying to run me down. At first they herd me back toward the rear of the train. I know my peril. Once to the rear of the train, it will pull out with me left behind. I double, and twist, and turn, dodge through my pursuers, and gain the front of the train. One shack still hangs on after me. All right, I'll give him the run of his life, for my wind is good. I run straight ahead along the track. It doesn't matter. If he chases me ten miles, he'll nevertheless have to catch the train, and I can board her at any speed that he can.

So I run on, keeping just comfortably ahead of him and straining my eyes in the gloom for cattle-guards and switches that may bring me to grief. Alas! I strain my eyes too far ahead, and trip over something just under my feet, I know not what, some little thing, and go down to earth in a long, stumbling fall. The next moment I am on my feet, but the shack has me by the collar. I do not struggle. I am busy with breathing deeply and with sizing him up. He is narrow-shouldered, and I have at least thirty pounds the better of him in weight. Besides, he is just as tired as I am, and if he tries to slug me, I'll teach him a few things.

But he doesn't try to slug me, and that problem is settled. Instead, he starts to lead me back toward the train, and another possible problem arises. I see the lanterns of the conductor and the other shack. We are approaching them. Not for nothing have I made the acquaintance of the New York police. Not for nothing, in box-cars, by water-tanks, and in prison-cells, have I listened to bloody tales of man-handling. What if these three men are about to man-handle me? Heaven knows I have given them provocation enough. I think quickly. We are drawing nearer and nearer to the other two trainmen. I line up the stomach and the jaw of my captor, and plan the right and left I'll give him at the first sign of trouble.

Pshaw! I know another trick I'd like to work on him, and I almost regret that I did not do it at the moment I was captured. I could make him sick, what of his clutch on my collar. His fingers, tight-gripping, are buried inside my collar. My coat is tightly buttoned. Did you ever see a tourniquet? Well, this is one. All I have to do is to duck my head under his arm and begin to twist. I must twist rapidly—very rapidly. I know how to do it; twisting in a violent, jerky way, ducking my head under his arm with each revolution. Before he knows it, those detaining fingers of his will be detained. He will be unable to withdraw them. It is a powerful leverage. Twenty seconds after I have started revolving, the blood will be bursting out of his finger-ends, the delicate tendons will be rupturing, and all the muscles and nerves will be mashing and crushing together in a shrieking mass. Try it sometime when somebody has you by the collar. But be quick—quick as lightning. Also, be sure to hug yourself while you are revolving—hug your face with your left arm and your abdomen with your right. You see, the other fellow might try to stop you with a punch from his free arm. It would be a good idea, too, to revolve away from that free arm rather than toward it. A punch going is never so bad as a punch coming.

That shack will never know how near he was to being made very, very sick. All that saves him is that it is not in their plan to manhandle me. When we draw near enough, he calls out that he has me, and they signal the train to come on. The engine passes us, and the three blinds. After that, the conductor and the other shack swing aboard. But still my captor holds on to me. I see the plan. He is going to hold me until the rear of the train goes by. Then he will hop on, and I shall be left behind—ditched.

But the train has pulled out fast, the engineer trying to make up for lost time. Also, it is a long train. It is going very lively, and I know the shack is measuring its speed with apprehension.

"Think you can make it?" I query innocently.

He releases my collar, makes a quick run, and swings aboard. A number of coaches are yet to pass by. He knows it, and remains on the steps, his head poked out and watching me. In that moment my next move comes to me. I'll make the last platform. I know she's going fast and faster, but I'll only get a roll in the dirt if I fail, and the optimism of youth is mine. I do not give myself away. I stand with a dejected droop of shoulder, advertising that I have abandoned hope. But at the same time I am feeling with my feet the good gravel. It is perfect footing. Also I am watching the poked-out head of the shack. I see it withdrawn. He is confident that the train is going too fast for me ever to make it.

And the train *is* going fast—faster than any train I have ever tackled. As the last coach comes by I sprint in the same direction with it. It is a swift, short sprint. I cannot hope to equal the speed of the train, but I can reduce the difference of our speed to the minimum, and, hence, reduce the shock of impact, when I leap on board. In the fleeting instant of darkness I do not see the iron hand-rail of the last platform; nor is there time for me to locate it. I reach for where I think it ought to be, and at the same instant my feet leave the ground. It is all in the toss. The next moment I may be rolling in the gravel with broken ribs, or arms, or head. But my fingers grip the handhold, there is a jerk on my arms that slightly pivots my body, and my feet land on the steps with sharp violence.

My fingers grip the handhold, and my feet land on the steps with sharp violence.

I sit down, feeling very proud of myself. In all my hoboing it is the best bit of train-jumping I have done. I know that late at night one is always good for several stations on the last platform, but I do not care to trust myself at the rear of the train. At the first stop I run forward on the off-side of the train, pass the Pullmans, and duck under and take a rod under a day-coach.[6] At the next stop I run forward again and take another rod.

I am now comparatively safe. The shacks think I am ditched. But the long day and the strenuous night are beginning to tell on me.

Also, it is not so windy nor cold underneath, and I begin to doze. This will never do. Sleep on the rods spells death, so I crawl out at a station and go forward to the second blind. Here I can lie down and sleep; and here I do sleep—how long I do not know—for I am awakened by a lantern thrust into my face. The two shacks are staring at me. I scramble up on the defensive, wondering as to which one is going to make the first "pass" at me. But slugging is far from their minds.

"I thought you was ditched," says the shack who had held me by the collar.

"If you hadn't let go of me when you did, you'd have been ditched along with me," I answer.

"How's that?" he asks.

"I'd have gone into a clinch with you, that's all," is my reply.

They hold a consultation, and their verdict is summed up in:—

"Well, I guess you can ride, Bo. There's no use trying to keep you off."

And they go away and leave me in peace to the end of their division.

I have given the foregoing as a sample of what "holding her down" means. Of course, I have selected a fortunate night out of my experiences, and said nothing of the nights—and many of them—when I was tripped up by accident and ditched.

In conclusion, I want to tell of what happened when I reached the end of the division. On single-track, transcontinental lines, the freight trains wait at the divisions and follow out after the passenger trains. When the division was reached, I left my train, and looked for the freight that would pull out behind it. I found the freight, made up on a side-track and waiting. I climbed into a box-car half full of coal and lay down. In no time I was asleep.

I was awakened by the sliding open of the door. Day was just dawning, cold and gray, and the freight had not yet started. A "con" (conductor) was poking his head inside the door.

"Get out of that, you blankety-blank-blank!" he roared at me.

I got, and outside I watched him go down the line inspecting every car in the train. When he got out of sight I thought to myself

I was awakened by the sliding open of the door.

that he would never think I'd have the nerve to climb back into the very car out of which he had fired me. So back I climbed and lay down again.

Now that con's mental processes must have been paralleling mine, for he reasoned that it was the very thing I would do. For back he came and fired me out.

Now, surely, I reasoned, he will never dream that I'd do it a third time. Back I went, into the very same car. But I decided to make sure. Only one side-door could be opened. The other side-door was nailed up. Beginning at the top of the coal, I dug a hole alongside of that door and lay down in it. I heard the other door open. The con climbed up and looked in over the top of the coal. He couldn't see me. He called to me to get out. I tried to fool him by remaining quiet. But when he began tossing chunks of coal into the hole on top of me, I gave up and for the third time was fired out. Also, he informed me in warm terms of what would happen to me if he caught me in there again.

I changed my tactics. When a man is paralleling your mental processes, ditch him. Abruptly break off your line of reasoning, and go off on a new line. This I did. I hid between some cars on an adjacent side-track, and watched. Sure enough, that con came back again to the car. He opened the door, he climbed up, he called, he threw coal into the hole I had made. He even crawled over the coal and looked into the hole. That satisfied him. Five minutes later the freight was pulling out, and he was not in sight. I ran alongside the car, pulled the door open, and climbed in. He never looked for me again, and I rode that coal-car precisely one thousand and twenty-two miles, sleeping most of the time and getting out at divisions (where the freights always stop for an hour or so) to beg my food. And at the end of the thousand and twenty-two miles I lost that car through a happy incident. I got a "set-down," and the tramp doesn't live who won't miss a train for a set-down any time.

PICTURES

"What do it matter where or 'ow we die,
So long as we've our 'ealth to watch it all?"
—*Sestina of the Tramp-Royal.*

Perhaps the greatest charm of tramp-life is the absence of monotony. In Hobo Land the face of life is protean—an ever changing phantasmagoria, where the impossible happens and the unexpected jumps out of the bushes at every turn of the road. The hobo never knows what is going to happen the next moment; hence, he lives only in the present moment. He has learned the futility of telic endeavor, and knows the delight of drifting along with the whimsicalities of Chance.

Often I think over my tramp days, and ever I marvel at the swift succession of pictures that flash up in my memory. It matters not where I begin to think; any day of all the days is a day apart, with a record of swift-moving pictures all its own. For instance, I remember a sunny summer morning in Harrisburg, Pennsylvania, and immediately comes to my mind the auspicious beginning of the day—a "set-down" with two maiden ladies, and not in their kitchen, but in their dining room, with them beside me at the table. We ate eggs, out of egg-cups! It was the first time I had ever seen egg-cups, or heard of egg-cups! I was a bit awkward at first, I'll confess; but I was hungry and unabashed. I mastered the egg-cup, and I mastered the eggs in a way that made those two maiden ladies sit up.

Why, they ate like a couple of canaries, dabbling with the one egg each they took, and nibbling at tiny wafers of toast. Life was low in

A "set-down" with two maiden ladies, with
them beside me at the table.

their bodies; their blood ran thin; and they had slept warm all night.
I had been out all night, consuming much fuel of my body to keep
warm, beating my way down from a place called Emporium, in the
northern part of the state. Wafers of toast! Out of sight! But each
wafer was no more than a mouthful to me—nay, no more than a
bite. It is tedious to have to reach for another piece of toast each bite
when one is potential with many bites.

When I was a very little lad, I had a very little dog called Punch.
I saw to his feeding myself. Some one in the household had shot a lot
of ducks, and we had a fine meat dinner. When I had finished, I prepared Punch's dinner—a large plateful of bones and tidbits. I went
outside to give it to him. Now it happened that a visitor had ridden
over from a neighboring ranch, and with him had come a Newfoundland dog as big as a calf. I set the plate on the ground. Punch

wagged his tail and began. He had before him a blissful half-hour at least. There was a sudden rush. Punch was brushed aside like a straw in the path of a cyclone, and that Newfoundland swooped down upon the plate. In spite of his huge maw he must have been trained to quick lunches, for, in the fleeting instant before he received the kick in the ribs I aimed at him, he completely engulfed the contents of the plate. He swept it clean. One last lingering lick of his tongue removed even the grease stains.

As that big Newfoundland behaved at the plate of my dog Punch, so behaved I at the table of those two maiden ladies of Harrisburg. I swept it bare. I didn't break anything, but I cleaned out the eggs and the toast and the coffee. The servant brought more, but I kept her busy, and ever she brought more and more. The coffee was delicious, but it needn't have been served in such tiny cups. What time had I to eat when it took all my time to prepare the many cups of coffee for drinking?

At any rate, it gave my tongue time to wag. Those two maiden ladies, with their pink-and-white complexions and gray curls, had never looked upon the bright face of adventure. As the "Tramp-Royal" would have it, they had worked all their lives "on one same shift." Into the sweet scents and narrow confines of their uneventful existence I brought the large airs of the world, freighted with the lusty smells of sweat and strife, and with the tangs and odors of strange lands and soils. And right well I scratched their soft palms with the callous on my own palms—the half-inch horn that comes of pull-and-haul of rope and long and arduous hours of caressing shovel-handles. This I did, not merely in the braggadocio of youth, but to prove, by toil performed, the claim I had upon their charity.

Ah, I can see them now, those dear, sweet ladies, just as I sat at their breakfast table twelve years ago, discoursing upon the way of my feet in the world, brushing aside their kindly counsel as a real devilish fellow should, and thrilling them, not alone with my own adventures, but with the adventures of all the other fellows with whom I had rubbed shoulders and exchanged confidences. I appropriated them all, the adventures of the other fellows, I mean; and if those maiden ladies had been less trustful and guileless, they could have tangled me up beautifully in my chronology. Well, well, and what of it? It was fair exchange. For their many cups of coffee, and eggs, and bites of toast, I gave full value. Right royally I gave them entertainment. My coming to sit at their table was their adventure, and adventure is beyond price anyway.

Coming along the street, after parting from the maiden ladies, I gathered in a newspaper from the doorway of some late-riser, and in a grassy park lay down to get in touch with the last twenty-four hours of the world. There, in the park, I met a fellow-hobo who told me his life-story and who wrestled with me to join the United States Army. He had given in to the recruiting officer and was just about to join, and he couldn't see why I shouldn't join with him. He had been a member of Coxey's Army in the march to Washington several months before, and that seemed to have given him a taste for army life. I, too, was a veteran, for had I not been a private in Company L of the Second Division of Kelly's Industrial Army? —said Company L being commonly known as the "Nevada push." But my army experience had had the opposite effect on me; so I left that hobo to go his way to the dogs of war, while I "threw my feet" for dinner.

This duty performed, I started to walk across the bridge over the Susquehanna to the west shore. I forget the name of the railroad that ran down that side, but while lying in the grass in the morning the idea had come to me to go to Baltimore; so to Baltimore I was going on that railroad, whatever its name was. It was a warm afternoon, and part way across the bridge I came to a lot of fellows who were in swimming off one of the piers. Off went my clothes and in went I. The water was fine; but when I came out and dressed, I found I had been robbed. Some one had gone through my clothes. Now I leave it to you if being robbed isn't in itself adventure enough for one day. I have known men who have been robbed and who have talked all the rest of their lives about it. True, the thief that went through my clothes didn't get much—some thirty or forty cents in nickels and pennies, and my tobacco and cigarette papers; but it was all I had, which is more than most men can be robbed of, for they have something left at home, while I had no home. It was a pretty tough gang in swimming there. I sized up, and knew better than to squeal. So I

I gathered in a newspaper from the doorway of some late-riser.

begged "the makings," and I could have sworn it was one of my own papers I rolled the tobacco in.

Then on across the bridge I hiked to the west shore. Here ran the railroad I was after. No station was in sight. How to catch a freight without walking to a station was the problem. I noticed that the track came up a steep grade, culminating at the point where I had tapped it, and I knew that a heavy freight couldn't pull up there any too lively. But how lively? On the opposite side of the track rose a high bank. On the edge, at the top, I saw a man's head sticking up from the grass. Perhaps he knew how fast the freights took the grade, and when the next one went south. I called out my questions to him, and he motioned to me to come up.

I obeyed, and when I reached the top, I found four other men lying in the grass with him. I took in the scene and knew them for

I came to a lot of fellows who were in swimming off one of the piers.

what they were—American gypsies. In the open space that extended back among the trees from the edge of the bank were several nondescript wagons. Ragged, half-naked children swarmed over the camp, though I noticed that they took care not to come near and bother the men-folk. Several lean, unbeautiful, and toil-degraded women were pottering about with camp-chores, and one I noticed who sat by herself on the seat of one of the wagons, her head drooped forward, her knees drawn up to her chin and clasped limply by her arms. She did not look happy. She looked as if she did not care for anything—in this I was wrong, for later I was to learn that there was something for which she did care. The full measure of human suffering was in her face, and, in addition, there was the tragic expression of incapacity for further suffering. Nothing could hurt any more, was what her face seemed to portray; but in this, too, I was wrong.

I lay in the grass on the edge of the steep and talked with the men-folk. We were kin—brothers. I was the American hobo, and they were the American gypsy. I knew enough of their argot for conversation, and they knew enough of mine. There were two more in their gang, who were across the river "mushing" in Harrisburg. A "musher" is an itinerant fakir. This word is not to be confounded with the Klondike "musher," though the origin of both terms may be the same; namely, the corruption of the French *marche ons,* to march, to walk, to "mush." The particular graft of the two mushers who had crossed the river was umbrella-mending; but what real graft lay behind their umbrella-mending, I was not told, nor would it have been polite to ask.

It was a glorious day. Not a breath of wind was stirring, and we basked in the shimmering warmth of the sun. From everywhere arose the drowsy hum of insects, and the balmy air was filled with scents of the sweet earth and the green growing things. We were too lazy to do more than mumble on in intermittent conversation. And then, all abruptly, the peace and quietude was jarred awry by man.

Two bare-legged boys of eight or nine in some minor way broke some rule of the camp—what it was I did not know; and a man who lay beside me suddenly sat up and called to them. He was chief of the tribe, a man with narrow forehead and narrow-slitted eyes, whose thin lips and twisted sardonic features explained why the two boys jumped and tensed like startled deer at the sound of his voice. The alertness of fear was in their faces, and they turned, in a panic, to run. He called to them to come back, and one boy lagged behind reluctantly, his meagre little frame portraying in pantomime the struggle within him between fear and reason. He wanted to come back. His intelligence and past experience told him that to come back was a lesser evil than to run on; but lesser evil that it was, it was great enough to put wings to his fear and urge his feet to flight.

Still he lagged and struggled until he reached the shelter of the trees, where he halted. The chief of the tribe did not pursue. He sauntered over to a wagon and picked up a heavy whip. Then he came back to the centre of the open space and stood still. He did not speak. He made no gestures. He was the Law, pitiless and omnipotent. He merely stood there and waited. And I knew, and all knew, and the two boys in the shelter of the trees knew, for what he waited.

The boy who had lagged slowly came back. His face was stamped with quivering resolution. He did not falter. He had made up his mind to take his punishment. And mark you, the punishment was not for the original offence, but for the offence of running away. And in this, that tribal chieftain but behaved as behaves the exalted society in which he lived. We punish our criminals, and when they escape and run away, we bring them back and add to their punishment.

Straight up to the chief the boy came, halting at the proper distance for the swing of the lash. The whip hissed through the air, and I caught myself with a start of surprise at the weight of the blow. The thin little leg was so very thin and little. The flesh showed white where the lash had curled and bitten, and then, where the white had shown, sprang up the savage welt, with here and there along its length little scarlet oozings where the skin had broken. Again the whip swung, and the boy's whole body winced in anticipation of the blow, though he did not move from the spot. His will held good. A second welt sprang up, and a third. It was not until the fourth landed that the boy screamed. Also, he could no longer stand still, and from then on, blow after blow, he danced up and down in his anguish, screaming; but he did not attempt to run away. If his involuntary dancing took him beyond the reach of the whip, he danced back into range again. And when it was all over—a dozen blows—he went away, whimpering and squealing, among the wagons.

The chief stood still and waited. The second boy came out from the trees. But he did not come straight. He came like a cringing dog, obsessed by little panics that made him turn and dart away for half a dozen steps. But always he turned and came back, circling nearer and nearer to the man, whimpering, making inarticulate animal-noises in his throat. I saw that he never looked at the man. His eyes always were fixed upon the whip, and in his eyes was a terror that made me sick—the frantic terror of an inconceivably maltreated child. I have seen strong men dropping right and left out of battle and squirming in their death-throes, I have seen them by scores blown into the air by bursting shells and their bodies torn asunder; believe me, the witnessing was as merrymaking and laughter and song to me in comparison with the way the sight of that poor child affected me.

The whipping began. The whipping of the first boy was as play compared with this one. In no time the blood was running down his thin little legs. He danced and squirmed and doubled up till it seemed almost that he was some grotesque marionette operated by strings. I say "seemed," for his screaming gave the lie to the seeming and stamped it with reality. His shrieks were shrill and piercing; within them no hoarse notes, but only the thin sexlessness of the voice of a child. The time came when the boy could stand it no more. Reason fled, and he tried to run away. But now the man followed up, curbing his flight, herding him with blows back always into the open space.

Then came interruption. I heard a wild smothered cry. The woman who sat in the wagon seat had got out and was running to interfere. She sprang between the man and boy.

"You want some, eh?" said he with the whip. "All right, then."

He swung the whip upon her. Her skirts were long, so he did not try for her legs. He drove the lash for her face, which she shielded as best she could with her hands and forearms, drooping her head forward between her lean shoulders, and on the lean shoulders and arms receiving the blows. Heroic mother! She knew just what she was doing. The boy, still shrieking, was making his get-away to the wagons.

And all the while the four men lay beside me and watched and made no move. Nor did I move, and without shame I say it; though my reason was compelled to struggle hard against my natural impulse to rise up and interfere. I knew life. Of what use to the woman, or to me, would be my being beaten to death by five men there on the bank of the Susquehanna? I once saw a man hanged, and though my whole soul cried protest, my mouth cried not. Had it cried, I should most likely have had my skull crushed by the butt of a revolver, for it was the law that the man should hang. And here, in this gypsy group, it was the law that the woman should be whipped.

Even so, the reason in both cases that I did not interfere was not that it was the law, but that the law was stronger than I. Had it not been for those four men beside me in the grass, right gladly would I have waded into the man with the whip. And, barring the accident of the landing on me with a knife or a club in the hands of some of the various women of the camp, I am confident that I should have beaten him into a mess. But the four men *were* beside me in the grass. They made their law stronger than I.

Oh, believe me, I did my own suffering. I had seen women beaten before, often, but never had I seen such a beating as this. Her dress across the shoulders was cut into shreds. One blow that had passed her guard, had raised a bloody welt from cheek to chin. Not one blow, nor two, not one dozen, nor two dozen, but endlessly, infinitely, that whip-lash smote and curled about her. The sweat poured from me, and I breathed hard, clutching at the grass with my hands until I strained it out by the roots. And all the time my reason kept whispering, "Fool! Fool!" That welt on the face nearly did for me. I started to rise to my feet; but the hand of the man next to me went out to my shoulder and pressed me down.

"Easy, pardner, easy," he warned me in a low voice. I looked at him. His eyes met mine unwaveringly. He was a large man, broad-shouldered and heavy-muscled; and his face was lazy, phlegmatic, slothful, withal kindly, yet without passion, and quite soulless—a dim soul, unmalicious, unmoral, bovine, and stubborn. Just an animal he was, with no more than a faint flickering of intelligence, a good-natured brute with the strength and mental caliber of a gorilla. His hand pressed heavily upon me, and I knew the weight of the muscles behind. I looked at the other brutes, two of them unperturbed and incurious, and one of them that gloated over the spectacle; and my reason came back to me, my muscles relaxed, and I sank down in the grass.

My mind went back to the two maiden ladies with whom I had had breakfast that morning. Less than two miles, as the crow flies, separated them from this scene. Here, in the windless day, under a beneficent sun, was a sister of theirs being beaten by a brother of mine. Here was a page of life they could never see—and better so, though for lack of seeing they would never be able to understand their sisterhood, nor themselves, nor know the clay of which they were made. For it is not given to woman to live in sweet-scented, narrow rooms and at the same time be a little sister to all the world.

The whipping was finished, and the woman, no longer screaming, went back to her seat in the wagon. Nor did the other women come to her—just then. They were afraid. But they came afterward, when a decent interval had elapsed. The man put the whip away and rejoined us, flinging himself down on the other side of me. He was breathing hard from his exertions. He wiped the sweat from his eyes on his coat-sleeve, and looked challengingly at me. I returned his look carelessly; what he had done was no concern of mine. I did not go away abruptly. I lay there half an hour longer, which, under the circumstances, was tact and etiquette. I rolled cigarettes from tobacco I borrowed from them, and when I slipped down the bank to the railroad, I was equipped with the necessary information for catching the next freight bound south.

Well, and what of it? It was a page out of life, that's all; and there are many pages worse, far worse, that I have seen. I have sometimes held forth (facetiously, so my listeners believed) that the chief distinguishing trait between man and the other animals is that man is the only animal that maltreats the females of his kind. It is something of which no wolf nor cowardly coyote is ever guilty. It is something that even the dog, degenerated by domestication, will not do. The dog still retains the wild instinct in this matter, while man has lost most of his wild instincts—at least, most of the good ones.

Worse pages of life than what I have described? Read the reports on child labor in the United States,—east, west, north, and south, it doesn't matter where,—and know that all of us, profit-mongers that we are, are typesetters and printers of worse pages of life than that mere page of wife-beating on the Susquehanna.

I went down the grade a hundred yards to where the footing beside the track was good. Here I could catch my freight as it pulled slowly up the hill, and here I found half a dozen hoboes waiting for the same purpose. Several were playing seven-up with an old pack of cards. I took a hand. A coon began to shuffle the deck.[1] He was fat, and young, and moon-faced. He beamed with good-nature. It fairly oozed from him. As he dealt the first card to me, he paused and said:—

"Say, Bo, ain't I done seen you befo'?"

"You sure have," I answered. "An' you didn't have those same duds on, either."

He was puzzled,

"D'ye remember Buffalo?" I queried.

Then he knew me, and with laughter and ejaculation hailed me as a comrade; for at Buffalo his clothes had been striped while he did his bit of time in the Erie County Penitentiary. For that matter, my clothes had been likewise striped, for I had been doing my bit of time, too.

The game proceeded, and I learned the stake for which we played. Down the bank toward the river descended a steep and narrow path that led to a spring some twenty-five feet beneath. We played on the edge of the bank. The man who was "stuck" had to take a small condensed-milk can, and with it carry water to the winners.

The first game was played and the coon was stuck. He took the small milk-tin and climbed down the bank, while we sat above and guyed him. We drank like fish. Four round trips he had to make for me alone, and the others were equally lavish with their thirst. The path was very steep, and sometimes the coon slipped when part way up, spilled the water, and had to go back for more. But he didn't get angry. He laughed as heartily as any of us; that was why he slipped so often. Also, he assured us of the prodigious quantities of water he would drink when some one else got stuck.

When our thirst was quenched, another game was started. Again the coon was stuck, and again we drank our fill. A third game and a fourth ended the same way, and each time that moon-faced darky nearly died with delight at appreciation of the fate that Chance was dealing out to him. And we nearly died with him, what of our delight. We laughed like careless children, or gods, there on the edge of the bank. I know that I laughed till it seemed the top of my head would come off, and I drank from the milk-tin till I was nigh water-logged. Serious discussion arose as to whether we could successfully board the freight when it pulled up the grade, what of the weight of water secreted on our persons. This particular phase of the situation just about finished the coon. He had to break off from water-carrying for at least five minutes while he lay down and rolled with laughter.

The lengthening shadows stretched farther and farther across the river, and the soft, cool twilight came on, and ever we drank water, and ever our ebony cup-bearer brought more and more. Forgotten was the beaten woman of the hour before. That was a page read and turned over; I was busy now with this new page, and when the engine whistled on the grade, this page would be finished and another begun; and so the book of life goes on, page after page and pages without end—when one is young.

And then we played a game in which the coon failed to be stuck. The victim was a lean and dyspeptic-looking hobo, the one who had laughed least of all of us. We said we didn't want any water—which was the truth. Not the wealth of Ormuz and of Ind, nor the pressure of a pneumatic ram, could have forced another drop into my saturated carcass.[2] The coon looked disappointed, then rose to the occasion and guessed he'd have some. He meant it, too. He had some, and then some, and then some. Ever the melancholy hobo climbed down and up the steep bank, and ever the coon called for more. He drank more water than all the rest of us put together. The twilight deepened into night, the stars came out, and he still drank on. I do believe that if the whistle of the freight hadn't sounded, he'd be there yet, swilling water and revenge while the melancholy hobo toiled down and up.

But the whistle sounded. The page was done. We sprang to our feet and strung out alongside the track. There she came, coughing and spluttering up the grade, the headlight turning night into day and silhouetting us in sharp relief. The engine passed us, and we were all running with the train, some boarding on the side-ladders, others "springing" the side-doors of empty box-cars and climbing in. I caught a flat-car loaded with mixed lumber and crawled away into a comfortable nook. I lay on my back with a newspaper under my head for a pillow. Above me the stars were winking and wheeling in squadrons back and forth as the train rounded the curves, and watching them I fell asleep. The day was done—one day of all my days. To-morrow would be another day, and I was young.

"PINCHED"

I rode into Niagara Falls in a "side-door Pullman," or, in common parlance, a box-car. A flat-car, by the way, is known amongst the fraternity as a "gondola," with the second syllable emphasized and pronounced long. But to return. I arrived in the afternoon and headed straight from the freight train to the falls. Once my eyes were filled with that wonder-vision of down-rushing water, I was lost. I could not tear myself away long enough to "batter" the "privates" (domiciles) for my supper. Even a "set-down" could not have lured me away. Night came on, a beautiful night of moonlight, and I lingered by the falls until after eleven. Then it was up to me to hunt for a place to "kip."

Even a "set-down" could not have lured me away.

"Kip," "doss," "flop," "pound your ear," all mean the same thing; namely, to sleep. Somehow, I had a "hunch" that Niagara Falls was a "bad" town for hoboes, and I headed out into the country. I climbed a fence and "flopped" in a field. John Law would never find me there, I flattered myself. I lay on my back in the grass and slept like a babe. It was so balmy warm that I woke up not once all night. But with the first gray daylight my eyes opened, and I remembered the wonderful falls. I climbed the fence and started down the road to have another look at them. It was early—not more than five o'clock—and not until eight o'clock could I begin to batter for my breakfast. I could spend at least three hours by the river. Alas! I was fated never to see the river nor the falls again.

I started down the road.

The town was asleep when I entered it. As I came along the quiet street, I saw three men coming toward me along the sidewalk. They were walking abreast. Hoboes, I decided, like myself, who had got up early. In this surmise I was not quite correct. I was only sixty-six and two-thirds per cent correct. The men on each side were hoboes all right, but the man in the middle wasn't. I directed my steps to the edge of the sidewalk in order to let the trio go by. But it didn't go by.

At some word from the man in the centre, all three halted, and he of the centre addressed me.

I piped the lay on the instant. He was a "fly-cop" and the two hoboes were his prisoners.[1] John Law was up and out after the early worm. I was a worm. Had I been richer by the experiences that were to befall me in the next several months, I should have turned and run like the very devil. He might have shot at me, but he'd have had to hit me to get me. He'd have never run after me, for two hoboes in the hand are worth more than one on the get-away. But like a dummy I stood still when he halted me. Our conversation was brief.

"What hotel are you stopping at?" he queried.

He had me. I wasn't stopping at any hotel, and, since I did not know the name of a hotel in the place, I could not claim residence in any of them. Also, I was up too early in the morning. Everything was against me.

"I just arrived," I said.

"Well, you turn around and walk in front of me, and not too far in front. There's somebody wants to see you."

I was "pinched." I knew who wanted to see me. With that "fly-cop" and the two hoboes at my heels, and under the direction of the former, I led the way to the city jail. There we were searched and our names registered. I have forgotten, now, under which name I was registered. I gave the name of Jack Drake, but when they searched me, they found letters addressed to Jack London. This caused trouble and required explanation, all of which has passed from my mind, and to this day I do not know whether I was pinched as Jack Drake or Jack London. But one or the other, it should be there to-day in the prison register of Niagara Falls. Reference can bring it to light. The time was somewhere in the latter part of June, 1894. It was only a few days after my arrest that the great railroad strike began.

From the office we were led to the "Hobo" and locked in. The "Hobo" is that part of a prison where the minor offenders are confined together in a large iron cage. Since hoboes constitute the principal division of the minor offenders, the aforesaid iron cage is called the Hobo. Here we met several hoboes who had already been pinched that morning, and every little while the door was unlocked and two or three more were thrust in on us. At last, when we totalled sixteen, we were led upstairs into the court-room. And now I shall faithfully describe what took place in that court-room, for know that my patriotic American citizenship there received a shock from which it has never fully recovered.

In the court-room were the sixteen prisoners, the judge, and two bailiffs. The judge seemed to act as his own clerk. There were no witnesses. There were no citizens of Niagara Falls present to look on and see how justice was administered in their community. The judge glanced at the list of cases before him and called out a name. A hobo stood up. The judge glanced at a bailiff. "Vagrancy, your Honor," said the bailiff. "Thirty days," said his Honor. The hobo sat down, and the judge was calling another name and another hobo was rising to his feet.

The trial of that hobo had taken just about fifteen seconds. The trial of the next hobo came off with equal celerity. The bailiff said, "Vagrancy, your Honor," and his Honor said, "Thirty days." Thus it went like clockwork, fifteen seconds to a hobo—and thirty days.

They are poor dumb cattle, I thought to myself. But wait till my turn comes; I'll give his Honor a "spiel." Part way along in the performance, his Honor, moved by some whim, gave one of us an opportunity to speak. As chance would have it, this man was not a genuine hobo. He bore none of the earmarks of the professional "stiff." Had he approached the rest of us, while waiting at a water-tank for a freight, we should have unhesitatingly classified him as a "gay-cat." Gay-cat is the synonym for tenderfoot in Hobo Land. This gay-cat was well along in years—somewhere around forty-five, I should judge. His shoulders were humped a trifle, and his face was seamed by weather-beat.

For many years, according to his story, he had driven team for some firm in (if I remember rightly) Lockport, New York.[2] The firm had ceased to prosper, and finally, in the hard times of 1893, had gone out of business. He had been kept on to the last, though toward the last his work had been very irregular. He went on and explained at length his difficulties in getting work (when so many were out of work) during the succeeding months. In the end, deciding that he would find better opportunities for work on the Lakes, he had started for Buffalo. Of course he was "broke," and there he was. That was all.

"Thirty days," said his Honor, and called another hobo's name.

Said hobo got up. "Vagrancy, your Honor," said the bailiff, and his Honor said, "Thirty days."

And so it went, fifteen seconds and thirty days to each hobo. The machine of justice was grinding smoothly. Most likely, considering how early it was in the morning, his Honor had not yet had his breakfast and was in a hurry.

But my American blood was up. Behind me were the many generations of my American ancestry. One of the kinds of liberty those ancestors of mine had fought and died for was the right of trial by jury. This was my heritage, stained sacred by their blood, and it devolved upon me to stand up for it. All right, I threatened to myself; just wait till he gets to me.

He got to me. My name, whatever it was, was called, and I stood up. The bailiff said, "Vagrancy, your Honor," and I began to talk. But the judge began talking at the same time, and he said, "Thirty days." I started to protest, but at that moment his Honor was calling the name of the next hobo on the list. His Honor paused long enough to say to me, "Shut up!" The bailiff forced me to sit down. And the next moment that next hobo had received thirty days and the succeeding hobo was just in process of getting his.

When we had all been disposed of, thirty days to each stiff, his Honor, just as he was about to dismiss us, suddenly turned to the teamster from Lockport—the one man he had allowed to talk.

"Why did you quit your job?" his Honor asked.

Now the teamster had already explained how his job had quit him, and the question took him aback.

"Your Honor," he began confusedly, "isn't that a funny question to ask?"

"Thirty days more for quitting your job," said his Honor, and the court was closed. That was the outcome. The teamster got sixty days all together, while the rest of us got thirty days.

We were taken down below, locked up, and given breakfast. It was a pretty good breakfast, as prison breakfasts go, and it was the best I was to get for a month to come.

As for me, I was dazed. Here was I, under sentence, after a farce of a trial wherein I was denied not only my right of trial by jury, but my right to plead guilty or not guilty. Another thing my fathers had fought for flashed through my brain—habeas corpus.[3] I'd show them. But when I asked for a lawyer, I was laughed at. Habeas corpus was all right, but of what good was it to me when I could communicate with no one outside the jail? But I'd show them. They couldn't keep me in jail forever. Just wait till I got out, that was all. I'd make them sit up. I knew something about the law and my own rights, and I'd expose their maladministration of justice. Visions of damage suits and sensational newspaper headlines were dancing before my eyes when the jailers came in and began hustling us out into the main office.

A policeman snapped a handcuff on my right wrist. (Ah, ha, thought I, a new indignity. Just wait till I get out.) On the left wrist of a negro he snapped the other handcuff of that pair. He was a very tall negro, well past six feet—so tall was he that when we stood side by side his hand lifted mine up a trifle in the manacles. Also, he was the happiest and the raggedest negro I have ever seen.

We were all handcuffed similarly, in pairs. This accomplished, a bright nickel-steel chain was brought forth, run down through the links of all the handcuffs, and locked at front and rear of the double-line. We were now a chain-gang. The command to march was given, and out we went upon the street, guarded by two officers. The tall negro and I had the place of honor. We led the procession.

After the tomb-like gloom of the jail, the outside sunshine was dazzling. I had never known it to be so sweet as now, a prisoner with clanking chains, I knew that I was soon to see the last of it for thirty days. Down through the streets of Niagara Falls we marched to the railroad station, stared at by curious passers-by, and especially by a group of tourists on the veranda of a hotel that we marched past.

There was plenty of slack in the chain, and with much rattling and clanking we sat down, two and two, in the seats of the smoking-car. Afire with indignation as I was at the outrage that had been perpetrated on me and my forefathers, I was nevertheless too prosaically practical to lose my head over it. This was all new to me. Thirty days of mystery were before me, and I looked about me to find somebody who knew the ropes. For I had already learned that I was not bound for a petty jail with a hundred or so prisoners in it, but for a full-grown penitentiary with a couple of thousand prisoners in it, doing anywhere from ten days to ten years.

In the seat behind me, attached to the chain by his wrist, was a squat, heavily-built, powerfully-muscled man. He was somewhere between thirty-five and forty years of age. I sized him up. In the corners of his eyes I saw humor and laughter and kindliness. As for the rest of him, he was a brute-beast, wholly unmoral, and with all the passion and turgid violence of the brute-beast. What saved him, what made him possible for me, were those corners of his eyes—the humor and laughter and kindliness of the beast when unaroused.

He was my "meat." I "cottoned" to him. While my cuff-mate, the tall negro, mourned with chucklings and laughter over some laundry he was sure to lose through his arrest, and while the train rolled on toward Buffalo, I talked with the man in the seat behind me. He had an empty pipe. I filled it for him with my precious tobacco— enough in a single filling to make a dozen cigarettes. Nay, the more we talked the surer I was that he was my meat, and I divided all my tobacco with him.

Now it happens that I am a fluid sort of an organism, with sufficient kinship with life to fit myself in 'most anywhere. I laid myself out to fit in with that man, though little did I dream to what extraordinary good purpose I was succeeding. He had never been in the particular penitentiary to which we were going, but he had done "one-," "two-," and "five-spots" in various other penitentiaries (a "spot" is a year), and he was filled with wisdom. We became pretty chummy, and my heart bounded when he cautioned me to follow his lead. He called me "Jack," and I called him "Jack."

The train stopped at a station about five miles from Buffalo, and we, the chain-gang, got off. I do not remember the name of this station, but I am confident that it is some one of the following: Rocklyn, Rockwood, Black Rock, Rockcastle, or Newcastle. But whatever the name of the place, we were walked a short distance and then put on a street-car. It was an old-fashioned car, with a seat, running the full length, on each side. All the passengers who sat on one side were asked to move over to the other side, and we, with a great clanking of chain, took their places. We sat facing them, I remember, and I remember, too, the awed expression on the faces of the women, who took us, undoubtedly, for convicted murderers and bank-robbers. I tried to look my fiercest, but that cuff-mate of mine, the too happy negro, insisted on rolling his eyes, laughing, and reiterating, "O Lawdy! Lawdy!"

We left the car, walked some more, and were led into the office of the Erie County Penitentiary. Here we were to register, and on that register one or the other of my names will be found. Also, we were informed that we must leave in the office all our valuables: money, tobacco, matches, pocket-knives, and so forth.

We were led into the office of the Penitentiary.

My new pal shook his head at me.

"If you do not leave your things here, they will be confiscated inside," warned the official.

Still my pal shook his head. He was busy with his hands, hiding his movements behind the other fellows. (Our handcuffs had been removed.) I watched him, and followed suit, wrapping up in a bundle in my handkerchief all the things I wanted to take in. These bundles the two of us thrust into our shirts. I noticed that our fellow-prisoners, with the exception of one or two who had watches, did not turn over their belongings to the man in the office. They were determined to smuggle them in somehow, trusting to luck; but they were not so wise as my pal, for they did not wrap their things in bundles.

Our erstwhile guardians gathered up the handcuffs and chain and departed for Niagara Falls, while we, under new guardians, were led away into the prison. While we were in the office, our number had been added to by other squads of newly arrived prisoners, so that we were now a procession forty or fifty strong.

Know, ye unimprisoned, that traffic is as restricted inside a large prison as commerce was in the Middle Ages. Once inside a penitentiary, one cannot move about at will. Every few steps are encountered great steel doors or gates which are always kept locked. We were bound for the barber-shop, but we encountered delays in the unlocking of doors for us. We were thus delayed in the first "hall" we entered. A "hall" is not a corridor. Imagine an oblong cube, built out of bricks and rising six stories high, each story a row of cells, say fifty cells in a row—in short, imagine a cube of colossal honeycomb. Place this cube on the ground and enclose it in a building with a roof overhead and walls all around. Such a cube and encompassing building constitute a "hall" in the Erie County Penitentiary. Also, to complete the picture, see a narrow gallery, with steel railing, running the full length of each tier of cells and at the ends of the oblong cube see all these galleries, from both sides, connected by a fire-escape system of narrow steel stairways.

We were halted in the first hall, waiting for some guard to unlock a door. Here and there, moving about, were convicts, with close-cropped heads and shaven faces, and garbed in prison stripes. One such convict I noticed above us on the gallery of the third tier of cells. He was standing on the gallery and leaning forward, his arms resting on the railing, himself apparently oblivious of our presence. He seemed staring into vacancy. My pal made a slight hissing noise. The

Each story a row of cells.

convict glanced down. Motioned signals passed between them. Then through the air soared the handkerchief bundle of my pal. The convict caught it, and like a flash it was out of sight in his shirt and he was staring into vacancy. My pal had told me to follow his lead. I watched my chance when the guard's back was turned, and my bundle followed the other one into the shirt of the convict.

A minute later the door was unlocked, and we filed into the barber-shop. Here were more men in convict stripes. They were the prison barbers. Also, there were bath-tubs, hot water, soap, and scrubbing-brushes. We were ordered to strip and bathe, each man to scrub his neighbor's back—a needless precaution, this compulsory bath, for the prison swarmed with vermin. After the bath, we were each given a canvas clothes-bag.

"Put all your clothes in the bags," said the guard. "It's no good trying to smuggle anything in. You've got to line up naked for inspection. Men for thirty days or less keep their shoes and suspenders. Men for more than thirty days keep nothing."

We filed into the barber shop.

This announcement was received with consternation. How could naked men smuggle anything past an inspection? Only my pal and I were safe. But it was right here that the convict barbers got in their work. They passed among the poor newcomers, kindly volunteering to take charge of their precious little belongings, and promising to return them later in the day. Those barbers were philanthropists—to hear them talk. As in the case of Fra Lippo Lippi, never was there such prompt disemburdening.[4] Matches, tobacco, rice-paper, pipes, knives, money, everything, flowed into the capacious shirts of the barbers. They fairly bulged with the spoil, and the guards made believe not to see. To cut the story short, nothing was ever returned. The barbers never had any intention of returning what they had taken. They considered it legitimately theirs. It was the barber-shop graft. There were many grafts in that prison, as I was to learn; and I, too, was destined to become a grafter—thanks to my new pal.

There were several chairs, and the barbers worked rapidly. The quickest shaves and hair-cuts I have ever seen were given in that shop. The men lathered themselves, and the barbers shaved them at the rate of a minute to a man. A hair-cut took a trifle longer. In three minutes the down of eighteen was scraped from my face, and my head was as smooth as a billiard-ball just sprouting a crop of bristles. Beards, mustaches, like our clothes and everything, came off. Take my word for it, we were a villainous-looking gang when they got through with us. I had not realized before how really altogether bad we were.

Then came the line-up, forty or fifty of us, naked as Kipling's heroes who stormed Lungtungpen.[5] To search us was easy. There were only our shoes and ourselves. Two or three rash spirits, who had doubted the barbers, had the goods found on them—which goods, namely, tobacco, pipes, matches, and small change, were quickly confiscated. This over, our new clothes were brought to us—stout prison shirts, and coats and trousers conspicuously striped. I had always lingered under the impression that the convict stripes were put on a man only after he had been convicted of a felony. I lingered no longer, but put on the insignia of shame and got my first taste of marching the lock-step.

In single file, close together, each man's hands on the shoulders of the man in front, we marched on into another large hall. Here we were ranged up against the wall in a long line and ordered to strip our left arms. A youth, a medical student who was getting in his practice on cattle such as we, came down the line. He vaccinated just about four times as rapidly as the barbers shaved. With a final caution to avoid rubbing our arms against anything, and to let the blood dry so as to form the scab, we were led away to our cells. Here my pal and I parted, but not before he had time to whisper to me, "Suck it out."

As soon as I was locked in, I sucked my arm clean. And afterward I saw men who had not sucked and who had horrible holes in their arms into which I could have thrust my fist. It was their own fault. They could have sucked.

In my cell was another man. We were to be cell-mates. He was a young, manly fellow, not talkative, but very capable, indeed as splendid a fellow as one could meet with in a day's ride, and this in spite of the fact that he had just recently finished a two-year term in some Ohio penitentiary.

Hardly had we been in our cell half an hour, when a convict sauntered down the gallery and looked in. It was my pal. He had the freedom of the hall, he explained. He was unlocked at six in the morning and not locked up again till nine at night. He was in with the "push" in that hall, and had been promptly appointed a trusty of the kind technically known as "hall-man." The man who had appointed him was also a prisoner and a trusty, and was known as "First Hall-man." There were thirteen hall-men in that hall. Ten of them had charge each of a gallery of cells, and over them were the First, Second, and Third Hall-men.

We newcomers were to stay in our cells for the rest of the day, my pal informed me, so that the vaccine would have a chance to take Then next morning we would be put to hard labor in the prison-yard.

"But I'll get you out of the work as soon as I can," he promised. "I'll get one of the hall-men fired and have you put in his place."

He put his hand into his shirt, drew out the handkerchief containing my precious belongings, passed it in to me through the bars, and went on down the gallery.

I opened the bundle. Everything was there. Not even a match was missing. I shared the makings of a cigarette with my cell-mate. When I started to strike a match for a light, he stopped me. A flimsy, dirty comforter lay in each of our bunks for bedding. He tore off a narrow strip of the thin cloth and rolled it tightly and telescopically into a long and slender cylinder. This he lighted with a precious match. The cylinder of tight-rolled cotton cloth did not flame. On the end a coal of fire slowly smouldered. It would last for hours, and my cell-mate called it a "punk." And when it burned short, all that was necessary was to make a new punk, put the end of it against the old, blow on them, and so transfer the glowing coal. Why, we could have given Prometheus pointers on the conserving of fire.[6]

At twelve o'clock dinner was served. At the bottom of our cage door was a small opening like the entrance of a runway in a chicken-yard. Through this were thrust two hunks of dry bread and two pannikins of "soup."[7] A portion of soup consisted of about a quart of hot water with floating on its surface a lonely drop of grease. Also, there was some salt in that water.

We drank the soup, but we did not eat the bread. Not that we were not hungry, and not that the bread was uneatable. It was fairly good bread. But we had reasons. My cell-mate had discovered that our cell was alive with bed-bugs. In all the cracks and interstices between the bricks where the mortar had fallen out flourished great colonies. The natives even ventured out in the broad daylight and swarmed over the walls and ceiling by hundreds. My cell-mate was wise in the ways of the beasts. Like Childe Roland, dauntless the slug-horn to his lips he bore.[8] Never was there such a battle. It lasted for hours. It was shambles. And when the last survivors fled to their brick-and-mortar fastnesses, our work was only half done. We chewed mouthfuls of our bread until it was reduced to the consistency of putty. When a fleeing belligerent escaped into a crevice between the bricks, we promptly walled him in with a daub of the chewed bread. We toiled on until the light grew dim and until every hole, nook, and cranny was closed. I shudder to think of the tragedies of starvation and cannibalism that must have ensued behind those bread-plastered ramparts.

We threw ourselves on our bunks, tired out and hungry, to wait for supper. It was a good day's work well done. In the weeks to come we at least should not suffer from the hosts of vermin. We had foregone our dinner, saved our hides at the expense of our stomachs; but we were content. Alas for the futility of human effort! Scarcely was our long task completed when a guard unlocked our door. A redistribution of prisoners was being made, and we were taken to another cell and locked in two galleries higher up.

Early next morning our cells were unlocked, and down in the hall the several hundred prisoners of us formed the lock-step and marched out into the prison-yard to go to work. The Erie Canal runs right by the back yard of the Erie County Penitentiary. Our task was to unload canal-boats, carrying huge stay-bolts on our shoulders, like railroad ties, into the prison.[9] As I worked I sized up the situation and studied the chances for a get-away. There wasn't the ghost of a show. Along the tops of the walls marched guards armed with repeating rifles, and I was told, furthermore, that there were machine-guns in the sentry-towers.

I did not worry. Thirty days were not so long. I'd stay those thirty days, and add to the store of material I intended to use, when I got out, against the harpies of justice. I'd show what an American boy could do when his rights and privileges had been trampled on the way mine

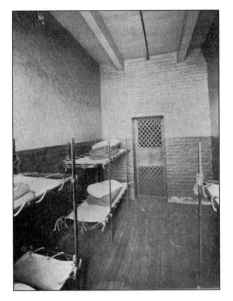

Our Bunks.

had. I had been denied my right of trial by jury; I had been denied my right to plead guilty or not guilty; I had been denied a trial even (for I couldn't consider that what I had received at Niagara Falls was a trial); I had not been allowed to communicate with a lawyer nor any one, and hence had been denied my right of suing for a writ of habeas corpus; my face had been shaved, my hair cropped close, convict stripes had been put upon my body; I was forced to toil hard on a diet of bread and water and to march the shameful lock-step with armed guards over me—and all for what? What had I done? What crime had I committed against the good citizens of Niagara Falls that all this vengeance should be wreaked upon me? I had not even violated their "sleeping-out" ordinance. I had slept outside their jurisdiction, in the country, that night. I had not even begged for a meal, or battered for a "light piece" on their streets. All that I had done was to walk along their sidewalk and gaze at their picayune waterfall. And what crime was there in that? Technically I was guilty of no misdemeanor. All right, I'd show them when I got out.

The next day I talked with a guard. I wanted to send for a lawyer. The guard laughed at me. So did the other guards. I really was *incommunicado* so far as the outside world was concerned. I tried to write a letter out, but I learned that all letters were read, and censured or confiscated, by the prison authorities, and that "short-timers" were not allowed to write letters anyway. A little later I tried smuggling letters out by men who were released, but I learned that they were searched and the letters found and destroyed. Never mind. It all helped to make it a blacker case when I did get out.

But as the prison days went by (which I shall describe in the next chapter), I "learned a few." I heard tales of the police, and police-courts, and lawyers, that were unbelievable and monstrous. Men, prisoners, told me of personal experiences with the police of great cities that were awful. And more awful were the hearsay tales they told me concerning men who had died at the hands of the police and who therefore could not testify for themselves. Years afterward, in the report of the Lexow Committee, I was to read tales true and more awful than those told to me.[10] But in the meantime, during the first days of my imprisonment, I scoffed at what I heard.

As the days went by, however, I began to grow convinced. I saw with my own eyes, there in that prison, things unbelievable and monstrous. And the more convinced I became, the profounder grew the respect in me for the sleuth-hounds of the law and for the whole institution of criminal justice.

My indignation ebbed away, and into my being rushed the tides of fear. I saw at last, clear-eyed, what I was up against. I grew meek and lowly. Each day I resolved more emphatically to make no rumpus when I got out. All I asked, when I got out, was a chance to fade away from the landscape. And that was just what I did do when I was released. I kept my tongue between my teeth, walked softly, and sneaked for Pennsylvania, a wiser and a humbler man.

THE PEN

For two days I toiled in the prison-yard. It was heavy work, and, in spite of the fact that I malingered at every opportunity, I was played out. This was because of the food. No man could work hard on such food. Bread and water, that was all that was given us. Once a week we were supposed to get meat; but this meat did not always go around, and since all nutriment had first been boiled out of it in the making of soup, it didn't matter whether one got a taste of it once a week or not.

Furthermore, there was one vital defect in the bread-and-water diet. While we got plenty of water, we did not get enough of the bread. A ration of bread was about the size of one's two fists, and

The Prison-yard.

three rations a day were given to each prisoner. There was one good thing, I must say, about the water—it was hot. In the morning it was called "coffee," at noon it was dignified as "soup," and at night it masqueraded as "tea." But it was the same old water all the time. The prisoners called it "water bewitched." In the morning it was black water, the color being due to boiling it with burnt bread-crusts. At noon it was served minus the color, with salt and a drop of grease added. At night it was served with a purplish-auburn hue that defied all speculation; it was darn poor tea, but it was dandy hot water.

We were a hungry lot in the Erie County Pen. Only the "long-timers" knew what it was to have enough to eat. The reason for this was that they would have died after a time on the fare we "short-timers" received. I know that the long-timers got more substantial grub, because there was a whole row of them on the ground floor in our hall, and when I was a trusty, I used to steal from their grub while serving them. Man cannot live on bread alone and not enough of it.

My pal delivered the goods. After two days of work in the yard I was taken out of my cell and made a trusty, a "hall-man." At morning and night we served the bread to the prisoners in their cells; but at twelve o'clock a different method was used. The convicts marched in from work in a long line. As they entered the door of our hall, they broke the lock-step and took their hands down from the shoulders of their line-mates. Just inside the door were piled trays of bread, and here also stood the First Hall-man and two ordinary hall-men. I was one of the two. Our task was to hold the trays of bread as the line of convicts filed past. As soon as the tray, say, that I was holding was emptied, the other hall-man took my place with a full tray. And when his was emptied, I took his place with a full tray. Thus the line tramped steadily by, each man reaching with his right hand and taking one ration of bread from the extended tray.

The task of the First Hall-man was different. He used a club. He stood beside the tray and watched. The hungry wretches could never get over the delusion that sometime they could manage to get two rations of bread out of the tray. But in my experience that sometime never came. The club of the First Hall-man had a way of flash-

Just inside the door were piled trays of bread.

ing out—quick as the stroke of a tiger's claw—to the hand that dared ambitiously. The First Hall-man was a good judge of distance, and he had smashed so many hands with that club that he had become infallible. He never missed, and he usually punished the offending convict by taking his one ration away from him and sending him to his cell to make his meal off of hot water.

And at times, while all these men lay hungry in their cells, I have seen a hundred or so extra rations of bread hidden away in the cells of the hall-men. It would seem absurd, our retaining this bread. But it was one of our grafts. We were economic masters inside our hall, turning the trick in ways quite similar to the economic masters of civilization. We controlled the food-supply of the population, and, just like our brother bandits outside, we made the people pay through the nose for it. We peddled the bread. Once a week, the men who worked in the yard received a five-cent plug of chewing tobacco. This chewing tobacco was the coin of the realm. Two or three rations of bread for a plug was the way we exchanged, and they traded, not because they loved tobacco less, but because they loved bread more. Oh, I know, it was like taking candy from a baby, but what would you? We had to live. And certainly there should be some reward for initiative and enterprise. Besides, we but patterned ourselves after our betters outside the walls, who, on a larger scale, and under the respectable disguise of merchants, bankers, and captains of industry, did precisely what we were doing. What awful things would have happened to those poor wretches if it hadn't been for us, I can't imagine. Heaven knows we put bread into circulation in the Erie County Pen. Ay, and we encouraged frugality and thrift . . . in the poor devils who forewent their tobacco. And then there was our example. In the breast of every convict there we implanted the ambition to become even as we and run a graft. Saviours of society—I guess yes.

Here was a hungry man without any tobacco. Maybe he was a profligate and had used it all up on himself. Very good; he had a pair of suspenders. I exchanged half a dozen rations of bread for it—or a dozen rations if the suspenders were very good. Now I never wore suspenders, but that didn't matter. Around the corner lodged a long-timer, doing ten years for manslaughter. He wore suspenders, and he wanted a pair. I could trade them to him for some of his meat. Meat was what I wanted. Or perhaps he had a tattered, paper-covered novel. That was treasure-trove. I could read it and then trade it off to the bakers for cake, or to the cooks for meat and vegetables, or to the firemen for decent coffee, or to some one or other for the newspaper that occasionally filtered in, heaven alone knows how. The cooks, bakers, and firemen were prisoners like myself, and they lodged in our hall in the first row of cells over us.

In short, a full-grown system of barter obtained in the Erie County Pen. There was even money in circulation. This money was sometimes smuggled in by the short-timers, more frequently came from the barber-shop graft, where the newcomers were mulcted, but most of all flowed from the cells of the long-timers—though how they got it I don't know.

What of his preëminent position, the First Hall-man was reputed to be quite wealthy. In addition to his miscellaneous grafts, he grafted on us. We farmed the general wretchedness, and the First Hall-man was Farmer-General over all of us. We held our particular grafts by his permission, and we had to pay for that permission, As I say, he was reputed to be wealthy; but we never saw his money, and he lived in a cell all to himself in solitary grandeur.

But that money was made in the Pen I had direct evidence, for I was cell-mate quite a time with the Third Hall-man. He had over sixteen dollars. He used to count his money every night after nine o'clock, when we were locked in. Also, he used to tell me each night what he would do to me if I gave away on him to the other hall-men. You see, he was afraid of being robbed, and danger threatened him from three different directions. There were the guards. A couple of them might jump upon him, give him a good beating for alleged insubordination, and throw him into the "solitaire" (the dungeon); and in the mix-up that sixteen dollars of his would take wings. Then again, the First Hall-man could have taken it all away from him by threatening to dismiss him and fire him back to hard labor in the prison-yard. And yet again, there were the ten of us who were ordinary hall-men. If we got an inkling of his wealth, there was a large liability, some quiet day, of the whole bunch of us getting him into a corner and dragging him down. Oh, we were wolves, believe me— just like the fellows who do business in Wall Street.

He had good reason to be afraid of us, and so had I to be afraid of him. He was a huge, illiterate brute, an ex-Chesapeake-Bay-oyster-pirate, an "ex-con" who had done five years in Sing Sing, and a general all-around stupidly carnivorous beast. He used to trap sparrows that flew into our hall through the open bars. When he made a capture, he hurried away with it into his cell, where I have seen him crunching bones and spitting out feathers as he bolted it raw. Oh, no, I never gave away on him to the other hall-men. This is the first time I have mentioned his sixteen dollars.

But I grafted on him just the same. He was in love with a woman prisoner who was confined in the "female department." He could neither read nor write, and I used to read her letters to him and write his replies. And I made him pay for it, too. But they were good letters. I laid myself out on them, put in my best licks, and furthermore, I won her for him; though I shrewdly guess that she was in love, not with him, but with the humble scribe. I repeat, those letters were great.

Another one of our grafts was "passing the punk." We were the celestial messengers, the fire-bringers, in that iron world of bolt and bar. When the men came in from work at night and were locked in their cells, they wanted to smoke. Then it was that we restored the divine spark, running the galleries, from cell to cell, with our smouldering punks. Those who were wise, or with whom we did business, had their punks all ready to light. Not every one got divine sparks, however. The guy who refused to dig up, went sparkless and smokeless to bed. But what did we care? We had the immortal cinch on him, and if he got fresh, two or three of us would pitch on him and give him "what-for."

You see, this was the working-theory of the hall-men. There were thirteen of us. We had something like half a thousand prisoners in our hall. We were supposed to do the work, and to keep order. The latter was the function of the guards, which they turned over to us. It was up to us to keep order; if we didn't, we'd be fired back to hard labor, most probably with a taste of the dungeon thrown in. But so long as we maintained order, that long could we work our own particular grafts.

Bear with me a moment and look at the problem. Here were thirteen beasts of us over half a thousand other beasts. It was a living hell, that prison, and it was up to us thirteen there to rule. It was impossible, considering the nature of the beasts, for us to rule by kindness. We ruled by fear. Of course, behind us, backing us up, were the guards. In extremity we called upon them for help; but it would bother them if we called upon them too often, in which event we could depend upon it that they would get more efficient trusties to take our places. But we did not call upon them often, except in a quiet sort of way, when we wanted a cell unlocked in order to get at a refractory prisoner inside. In such cases all the guard did was to unlock the door and walk away so as not to be a witness of what happened when half a dozen hall-men went inside and did a bit of man-handling.

As regards the details of this man-handling I shall say nothing. And after all, man-handling was merely one of the very minor unprintable horrors of the Erie County Pen. I say "unprintable"; and in justice I must also say "unthinkable." They were unthinkable to me until I saw them, and I was no spring chicken in the ways of the

All the guard did was to unlock the door.

world and the awful abysses of human degradation. It would take a deep plummet to reach bottom in the Erie County Pen, and I do but skim lightly and facetiously the surface of things as I there saw them.

At times, say in the morning when the prisoners came down to wash, the thirteen of us would be practically alone in the midst of them, and every last one of them had it in for us. Thirteen against five hundred, and we ruled by fear. We could not permit the slightest infraction of rules, the slightest insolence. If we did, we were lost. Our own rule was to hit a man as soon as he opened his mouth—hit him hard, hit him with anything. A broom-handle, end-on, in the face, had a very sobering effect. But that was not all. Such a man must be made an example of; so the next rule was to wade right in and follow him up. Of course, one was sure that every hall-man in sight would come on the run to join in the chastisement; for this also was a rule. Whenever any hall-man was in trouble with a prisoner, the duty of any other hall-man who happened to be around was to lend a fist. Never mind the merits of the case—wade in and hit, and hit with anything; in short, lay the man out.

I remember a handsome young mulatto of about twenty who got the insane idea into his head that he should stand for his rights. And he did have the right of it, too; but that didn't help him any. He lived on the topmost gallery. Eight hall-men took the conceit out of him in just about a minute and a half—for that was the length of time required to travel along his gallery to the end and down five flights of steel stairs. He travelled the whole distance on every portion of his anatomy except his feet, and the eight hall-men were not idle. The mulatto struck the pavement where I was standing watching it all. He regained his feet and stood upright for a moment. In that moment he threw his arms wide apart and omitted an awful scream of terror and pain and heartbreak. At the same instant, as in a transformation scene, the shreds of his stout prison clothes fell from him, leaving him wholly naked and streaming blood from every portion of the surface of his body. Then he collapsed in a heap, unconscious. He had learned his lesson, and every convict within those walls who heard him scream had learned a lesson. So had I learned mine. It is not a nice thing to see a man's heart broken in a minute and a half.

The following will illustrate how we drummed up business in the graft of passing the punk. A row of newcomers is installed in your cells. You pass along before the bars with your punk. "Hey, Bo, give us a light," some one calls to you. Now this is an advertisement that that particular man has tobacco on him. You pass in the punk and go your way. A little later you come back and lean up casually against the bars. "Say, Bo, can you let us have a little tobacco?" is what you say. If he is not wise to the game, the chances are that he solemnly avers that he hasn't any more tobacco. All very well. You condole with him and go your way. But you know that his punk will last him only the rest of that day. Next day you come by, and he says again, "Hey, Bo, give us a light." And you say, "You haven't any tobacco and you don't need a light." And you don't give him any, either. Half an hour after, or an hour or two or three hours, you will be passing by and the man will call out to you in mild tones, "Come here, Bo."

And you come. You thrust your hand between the bars and have it filled with precious tobacco. Then you give him a light.

Sometimes, however, a newcomer arrives, upon whom no grafts are to be worked. The mysterious word is passed along that he is to be treated decently. Where this word originated I could never learn. The one thing patent is that the man has a "pull." It may be with one of the superior hall-men; it may be with one of the guards in some other part of the prison; it may be that good treatment has been purchased from grafters higher up; but be it as it may, we know that it is up to us to treat him decently if we want to avoid trouble.

We hall-men were middle-men and common carriers. We arranged trades between convicts confined in different parts of the prison, and we put through the exchange. Also, we took our commissions coming and going. Sometimes the objects traded had to go through the hands of half a dozen middle-men, each of whom took his whack, or in some way or another was paid for his service.

Sometimes one was in debt for services, and sometimes one had others in his debt. Thus, I entered the prison in debt to the convict who smuggled in my things for me. A week or so afterward, one of the firemen passed a letter into my hand. It had been given to him by a barber. The barber had received it from the convict who had smuggled in my things. Because of my debt to him I was to carry the letter on. But he had not written the letter. The original sender was a long-timer in his hall. The letter was for a woman prisoner in the female department. But whether it was intended for her, or whether she, in turn, was one of the chain of go-betweens, I did not know. All that I knew was her description, and that it was up to me to get it into her hands.

Two days passed, during which time I kept the letter in my possession; then the opportunity came. The women did the mending of all the clothes worn by the convicts. A number of our hall-men had to go to the female department to bring back huge bundles of clothes. I fixed it with the First Hall-man that I was to go along. Door after door was unlocked for us as we threaded our way across the prison to the women's quarters. We entered a large room where the women sat working at their mending. My eyes were peeled for the woman who had been described to me. I located her and worked near to her. Two eagle-eyed matrons were on watch. I held the letter in my palm, and I looked my intention at the woman. She knew I had something for her; she must have been expecting it, and had set herself to divining, at the moment we entered, which of us was the messenger. But one of the matrons stood within two feet of her. Already the hall-men were picking up the bundles they were to carry away. The moment was passing. I delayed with my bundle, making believe that it was not tied securely. Would that matron ever look away? Or was I to fail? And just then another woman cut up playfully with one of the hall-men—stuck out her foot and tripped him, or pinched him, or did something or other. The matron looked that way and reprimanded the woman sharply. Now I do not know whether or not this was all planned to distract the matron's attention, but I did know that it was my opportunity. My particular woman's hand dropped from her lap down by her side. I stooped to pick up my bundle. From my stooping position I slipped the letter into her hand, and received another in exchange. The next moment the bundle was on my shoulder, the matron's gaze had returned to me because I was the last hall-man, and I was hastening to catch up with my companions. The letter I had received from the woman I turned over to the fireman, and thence it passed through the hands of the barber, of the convict who had smuggled in my things, and on to the long-timer at the other end.

Often we conveyed letters, the chain of communication of which was so complex that we knew neither sender nor sendee. We were but links in the chain. Somewhere, somehow, a convict would thrust a letter into my hand with the instruction to pass it on to the next link. All such acts were favors to be reciprocated later on, when I should be acting directly with a principal in transmitting letters, and from whom I should be receiving my pay. The whole prison was covered by a network of lines of communication. And we who were in control of the system of communication, naturally, since we were modelled after capitalistic society, exacted heavy tolls from our customers. It was service for profit with a vengeance, though we were at times not above giving service for love.

I stooped to pick up my bundle.

And all the time I was in the Pen I was making myself solid with my pal. He had done much for me, and in return he expected me to do as much for him. When we got out, we were to travel together, and, it goes without saying, pull off "jobs" together. For my pal was a criminal—oh, not a jewel of the first water, merely a petty criminal who would steal and rob, commit burglary, and, if cornered, not stop short of murder.[1] Many a quiet hour we sat and talked together. He had two or three jobs in view for the immediate future, in which my work was cut out for me, and in which I joined in planning the details. I had been with and seen much of criminals, and my pal never dreamed that I was only fooling him, giving him a string thirty days long. He thought I was the real goods, liked me because I was not stupid, and liked me a bit, too, I think, for myself. Of course I had not the slightest intention of joining him in a life of sordid, petty crime; but I'd have been an idiot to throw away all the good things his friendship made possible. When one is on the hot lava of hell, he cannot pick and choose his path, and so it was with me in the Erie County Pen. I had to stay in with the "push," or do hard labor on bread and water; and to stay in with the push I had to make good with my pal.

Life was not monotonous in the Pen. Every day something was happening: men were having fits, going crazy, fighting, or the hall-men were getting drunk. Rover Jack, one of the ordinary hall-men, was our star "oryide."[2] He was a true "profesh," a "blowed-in-the-glass" stiff, and as such received all kinds of latitude from the hall-men in authority. Pittsburg Joe, who was Second Hall-man, used to join Rover Jack in his jags; and it was a saying of the pair that the Erie County Pen was the only place where a man could get "slopped" and not be arrested. I never knew, but I was told that bromide of potassium, gained in devious ways from the dispensary, was the dope they used. But I do know, whatever their dope was, that they got good and drunk on occasion.

Our hall was a common stews, filled with the ruck and the filth, the scum and dregs, of society—hereditary inefficients, degenerates, wrecks, lunatics, addled intelligences, epileptics, monsters, weaklings, in short, a very nightmare of humanity. Hence, fits flourished with us. These fits seemed contagious. When one man began throwing a fit, others followed his lead. I have seen seven men down with fits at the same time, making the air hideous with their cries, while as many more lunatics would be raging and gibbering up and down. Nothing was ever done for the men with fits except to throw cold water on them. It was useless to send for the medical student or the doctor. They were not to be bothered with such trivial and frequent occurrences.

There was a young Dutch boy, about eighteen years of age, who had fits most frequently of all. He usually threw one every day. It was for that reason that we kept him on the ground floor farther down in the row of cells in which we lodged. After he had had a few fits in the prison-yard, the guards refused to be bothered with him any more, and so he remained locked up in his cell all day with a Cockney cell-mate, to keep him company. Not that the Cockney was of any use. Whenever the Dutch boy had a fit, the Cockney became paralyzed with terror.

The Dutch boy could not speak a word of English. He was a farmer's boy, serving ninety days as punishment for having got into a scrap with some one. He prefaced his fits with howling. He howled like a wolf. Also, he took his fits standing up, which was very inconvenient for him, for his fits always culminated in a headlong pitch to the floor. Whenever I heard the long wolf-howl rising, I used to grab a broom and run to his cell. Now the trusties were not allowed keys to the cells, so I could not get in to him. He would stand up in the middle of his narrow cell, shivering convulsively, his eyes rolled backward till only the whites were visible, and howling like a lost soul. Try as I would, I could never get the Cockney to lend him a hand. While he stood and howled, the Cockney crouched and trembled in the upper bunk, his terror-stricken gaze fixed on that awful figure, with eyes rolled back, that howled and howled. It was hard on him, too, the poor devil of a Cockney. His own reason was not any too firmly seated, and the wonder is that he did not go mad.

All that I could do was my best with the broom. I would thrust it through the bars, train it on Dutchy's chest, and wait. As the crisis approached he would begin swaying back and forth. I followed this swaying with the broom, for there was no telling when he would take that dreadful forward pitch. But when he did, I was there with the broom, catching him and easing him down. Contrive as I would, he never came down quite gently, and his face was usually bruised by the stone floor. Once down and writhing in convulsions, I'd throw a bucket of water over him. I don't know whether cold water was the right thing or not, but it was the custom in the Erie County Pen. Nothing more than that was ever done for him. He would lie there, wet, for an hour or so, and then crawl into his bunk. I knew better than to run to a guard for assistance. What was a man with a fit, anyway?

In the adjoining cell lived a strange character—a man who was doing sixty days for eating swill out of Barnum's swill-barrel, or at least that was the way he put it. He was a badly addled creature, and, at first, very mild and gentle. The facts of his case were as he had stated them. He had strayed out to the circus ground, and, being hungry, had made his way to the barrel that contained the refuse from the table of the circus people. "And it *was* good bread," he often assured me; "and the meat was out of sight." A policeman had seen him and arrested him, and there he was.

Once I passed his cell with a piece of stiff thin wire in my hand. He asked me for it so earnestly that I passed it through the bars to him. Promptly, and with no tool but his fingers, he broke it into short lengths and twisted them into half a dozen very creditable safety pins. He sharpened the points on the stone floor. Thereafter I did quite a trade in safety pins. I furnished the raw material and peddled the finished product, and he did the work. As wages, I paid him extra rations of bread, and once in a while a chunk of meat or a piece of soup-bone with some marrow inside.

But his imprisonment told on him, and he grew violent day by day. The hall-men took delight in teasing him. They filled his weak brain with stories of a great fortune that had been left him. It was in order to rob him of it that he had been arrested and sent to jail. Of course, as he himself knew, there was no law against eating out of a barrel. Therefore he was wrongly imprisoned. It was a plot to deprive him of his fortune.

The first I knew of it, I heard the hall-men laughing about the string they had given him. Next he held a serious conference with me, in which he told me of his millions and the plot to deprive him of them, and in which he appointed me his detective. I did my best to let him down gently, speaking vaguely of a mistake, and that it was another man with a similar name who was the rightful heir. I left him quite cooled down; but I couldn't keep the hall-men away from him, and they continued to string him worse than ever. In the end, after a most violent scene, he threw me down, revoked my private detectiveship, and went on strike. My trade in safety pins ceased. He refused to make any more safety pins, and he peppered me with raw material through the bars of his cell when I passed by.

I could never make it up with him. The other hall-men told him that I was a detective in the employ of the conspirators. And in the meantime the hall-men drove him mad with their stringing. His fictitious wrongs preyed upon his mind, and at last he became a dangerous and homicidal lunatic. The guards refused to listen to his tale of stolen millions, and he accused them of being in the plot. One day he threw a pannikin of hot tea over one of them, and then his case was investigated. The warden talked with him a few minutes through the bars of his cell. Then he was taken away for examination before the doctors. He never came back, and I often wonder if he is dead, or if he still gibbers about his millions in some asylum for the insane.

At last came the day of days, my release. It was the day of release for the Third Hall-man as well, and the short-timer girl I had won for him was waiting for him outside the wall. They went away blissfully together. My pal and I went out together, and together we walked down into Buffalo. Were we not to be together always? We

A few minutes later I was on board a freight.

begged together on the "main-drag" that day for pennies, and what we received was spent for "shupers" of beer—I don't know how they are spelled, but they are pronounced the way I have spelled them, and they cost three cents. I was watching my chance all the time for a get-away. From some bo on the drag I managed to learn what time a certain freight pulled out. I calculated my time accordingly. When the moment came, my pal and I were in a saloon. Two foaming shupers were before us. I'd have liked to say good-by. He had been good to me. But I did not dare. I went out through the rear of the saloon and jumped the fence. It was a swift sneak, and a few minutes later I was on board a freight and heading south on the Western New York and Pennsylvania Railroad.

HOBOES THAT PASS IN THE NIGHT

In the course of my tramping I encountered hundreds of hoboes, whom I hailed or who hailed me, and with whom I waited at water-tanks, "boiled-up," cooked "mulligans," "battered" the "drag" or "privates," and beat trains, and who passed and were seen never again. On the other hand, there were hoboes who passed and repassed with amazing frequency, and others, still, who passed like ghosts, close at hand, unseen, and never seen.

It was one of the latter that I chased clear across Canada over three thousand miles of railroad, and never once did I lay eyes on him. His "monica" was Skysail Jack.[1] I first ran into it at Montreal. Carved with a jack-knife was the skysail-yard of a ship. It was perfectly executed. Under it was "Skysail Jack." Above was "B.W. 9-15-94." This latter conveyed the information that he had passed through Montreal bound west, on October 15, 1894.[2] He had one day the start of me. "Sailor Jack" was my monica at that particular time, and promptly I carved it alongside of his, along with the date and the information that I, too, was bound west.

I had misfortune in getting over the next hundred miles, and eight days later I picked up Skysail Jack's trail three hundred miles west of Ottawa. There it was, carved on a water-tank, and by the date I saw that he likewise had met with delay. He was only two days ahead of me. I was a "comet" and "tramp-royal," so was Skysail Jack; and it was up to my pride and reputation to catch up with him. I "railroaded" day and night, and I passed him; then turn about he passed me. Sometimes he was a day or so ahead, and sometimes I was. From hoboes, bound east, I got word of him occasionally, when he happened to be ahead;

and from them I learned that he had become interested in Sailor Jack and was making inquiries about me.

We'd have made a precious pair, I am sure, if we'd ever got together; but get together we couldn't. I kept ahead of him clear across Manitoba, but he led the way across Alberta, and early one bitter gray morning, at the end of a division just east of Kicking Horse Pass, I learned that he had been seen the night before between Kicking Horse Pass and Rogers' Pass. It was rather curious the way the information came to me. I had been riding all night in a "side-door Pullman" (box-car), and nearly dead with cold had crawled out at the division to beg for food. A freezing fog was drifting past, and I "hit" some firemen I found in the round-house. They fixed me up with the leavings from their lunch-pails, and in addition I got out of them nearly a quart of heavenly "Java" (coffee). I heated the latter, and, as I sat down to eat, a freight pulled in from the west. I saw a side-door open and a road-kid climb out. Through the drifting fog he limped over to me. He was stiff with cold, his lips blue. I shared my Java and grub with him, learned about Skysail Jack, and then learned about him. Behold, he was from my own town, Oakland, California, and he was a member of the celebrated Boo Gang—a gang with which I had affiliated at rare intervals. We talked fast and bolted the grub in the half-hour that followed. Then my freight pulled out, and I was on it, bound west on the trail of Skysail Jack.

I was delayed between the passes, went two days without food, and walked eleven miles on the third day before I got any, and yet I succeeded in passing Skysail Jack along the Fraser River in British Columbia. I was riding "passengers" then and making time; but he must have been riding passengers, too, and with more luck or skill than I, for he got into Mission ahead of me.

Now Mission was a junction, forty miles east of Vancouver. From the junction one could proceed south through Washington and Oregon over the Northern Pacific. I wondered which way Skysail Jack would go, for I thought I was ahead of him. As for myself I was still bound west to Vancouver. I proceeded to the water-tank to leave that information, and there, freshly carved, with that day's date upon it, was Skysail Jack's monica. I hurried on into Vancouver. But he was gone. He had taken ship immediately and was still flying west on his world-adventure. Truly, Skysail Jack, you were a tramp-royal, and your mate was the "wind that tramps the world." I take off my hat to you. You were "blowed-in-the-glass" all right. A week later I, too, got my ship, and on board the steamship *Umatilla,* in the forecastle, was working my way down the coast to San Francisco. Skysail Jack and Sailor Jack—gee! if we'd ever got together.

Water-tanks are tramp directories. Not all in idle wantonness do tramps carve their monicas, dates, and courses. Often and often have I met hoboes earnestly inquiring if I had seen anywhere such and such a "stiff" or his monica. And more than once I have been able to give the monica of recent date, the water-tank, and the direction in which he was then bound. And promptly the hobo to whom I gave the information lit out after his pal. I have met hoboes who, in trying to catch a pal, had pursued clear across the continent and back again, and were still going.

"Monicas" are the *nom-de-rails* that hoboes assume or accept when thrust upon them by their fellows. Leary Joe, for instance, was timid, and was so named by his fellows. No self-respecting hobo would select Stew Bum for himself. Very few tramps care to remember their pasts during which they ignobly worked, so monicas based upon trades are very rare, though I remember having met the following: Moulder Blackey, Painter Red, Chi Plumber, Boiler-maker, Sailor Boy, and Printer Bo. "Chi" (pronounced *shy*), by the way, is the argot for "Chicago."

A favorite device of hoboes is to base their monicas on the localities from which they hail, as: New York Tommy, Pacific Slim, Buffalo Smithy, Canton Tim, Pittsburg Jack, Syracuse Shine, Troy Mickey, K. L. Bill, and Connecticut Jimmy. Then there was "Slim Jim from Vinegar Hill, who never worked and never will." A "shine" is always a negro, so called, possibly, from the high lights on his countenance. Texas Shine or Toledo Shine convey both race and nativity.

Among those that incorporated their race, I recollect the following: Frisco Sheeny, New York Irish, Michigan French, English Jack, Cockney Kid, and Milwaukee Dutch. Others seem to take their monicas in part from the color-schemes stamped upon them at birth, such as: Chi Whitey, New Jersey Red, Boston Blackey, Seattle Browney, and Yellow Dick and Yellow Belly—the last a Creole from Mississippi, who, I suspect, had his monica thrust upon him.

Texas Royal, Happy Joe, Bust Connors, Burley Bo, Tornado Blackey, and Touch McCall used more imagination in rechristening themselves. Others, with less fancy, carry the names of their physical peculiarities, such as: Vancouver Slim, Detroit Shorty, Ohio Fatty, Long Jack, Big Jim, Little Joe, New York Blink, Chi Nosey, and Broken-backed Ben.

By themselves come the road-kids, sporting an infinite variety of monicas. For example, the following, whom here and there I have encountered: Buck Kid, Blind Kid, Midget Kid, Holy Kid, Bat Kid, Swift Kid, Cookey Kid, Monkey Kid, Iowa Kid, Corduroy Kid, Orator Kid (who could tell how it happened), and Lippy Kid (who was insolent, depend upon it).

On the water-tank at San Marcial, New Mexico, a dozen years ago, was the following hobo bill of fare:—

(1) Main-drag fair.
(2) Bulls not hostile.
(3) Round-house good for kipping.
(4) North-bound trains no good.
(5) Privates no good.
(6) Restaurants good for cooks only.
(7) Railroad House good for night-work only.

Number one conveys the information that begging for money on the main street is fair; number two, that the police will not bother hoboes; number three, that one can sleep in the round-house. Number four, however, is ambiguous. The north-bound trains may be no good to beat, and they may be no good to beg. Number five means that the residences are not good to beggars, and number six means that only hoboes that have been cooks can get grub from the restaurants. Number seven bothers me. I cannot make out whether the Railroad House is a good place for any hobo to beg at night, or whether it is good only for hobo-cooks to beg at night, or whether any hobo, cook or non-cook, can lend a hand at night, helping the cooks of the Railroad House with their dirty work and getting something to eat in payment.

But to return to the hoboes that pass in the night. I remember one I met in California. He was a Swede, but he had lived so long in the United States that one couldn't guess his nationality. He had to tell it on himself. In fact, he had come to the United States when no more than a baby. I ran into him first at the mountain town of Truckee. "Which way, Bo?" was our greeting, and "Bound east" was the answer each of us gave. Quite a bunch of "stiffs" tried to ride out the overland that night, and I lost the Swede in the shuffle. Also, I lost the overland.

I arrived in Reno, Nevada, in a box-car that was promptly sidetracked. It was Sunday morning, and after I threw my feet for breakfast, I wandered over to the Piute camp to watch the Indians gambling. And there stood the Swede, hugely interested. Of course we got together. He was the only acquaintance I had in that region, and I was his only acquaintance. We rushed together like a couple of dissatisfied hermits, and together we spent the day, threw our feet for dinner, and late in the afternoon tried to "nail" the same freight. But he was ditched, and I rode her out alone, to be ditched myself in the desert twenty miles beyond.

Of all desolate places, the one at which I was ditched was the limit. It was called a flag-station, and it consisted of a shanty dumped inconsequentially into the sand and sage-brush. A chill wind was blowing, night was coming on, and the solitary telegraph operator who lived in the shanty was afraid of me. I knew that neither grub nor bed could I get out of him. It was because of his manifest fear of me that I did not believe him when he told me that east-bound trains never stopped there. Besides, hadn't I been thrown off of an east-bound train right at that very spot not five minutes before? He assured me that it had stopped under orders, and that a year might go by before another was stopped under orders. He advised me that it was only a dozen or fifteen miles on to Wadsworth and that I'd better hike. I elected to wait, however, and I had the pleasure of seeing two west-bound freights go by without stopping, and one east-bound freight. I wondered if the Swede was on the latter. It was up to me to hit the ties to Wadsworth, and hit them I did, much to the telegraph operator's relief, for I neglected to burn his shanty and murder him. Telegraph operators have much to be thankful for. At the end of half a dozen miles, I had to get off the ties and let the east-bound overland go by. She was going fast, but I caught sight of a dim form on the first "blind" that looked like the Swede.

That was the last I saw of him for weary days. I hit the high places across those hundreds of miles of Nevada desert, riding the overlands at night, for speed, and in the day-time riding in box-cars and getting my sleep. It was early in the year, and it was cold in those upland pastures. Snow lay here and there on the level, all the mountains were shrouded in white, and at night the most miserable wind imaginable blew off from them. It was not a land in which to linger. And remember, gentle reader, the hobo goes through such a land, without shelter, without money, begging his way and sleeping at night without blankets. This last is something that can be realized only by experience.

In the early evening I came down to the depot at Ogden. The overland of the Union Pacific was pulling east, and I was bent on making connections. Out in the tangle of tracks ahead of the engine I encountered a figure slouching through the gloom. It was the Swede. We shook hands like long-lost brothers, and discovered that our hands were gloved. "Where'd ye glahm 'em?" I asked. "Out of an engine-cab," he answered; "and where did you?" "They belonged to a fireman," said I; "he was careless."

We caught the blind as the overland pulled out, and mighty cold we found it. The way led up a narrow gorge between snow-covered mountains, and we shivered and shook and exchanged confidences about how we had covered the ground between Reno and Ogden. I had closed my eyes for only an hour or so the previous night, and the blind was not comfortable enough to suit me for a snooze. At a stop, I went forward to the engine. We had on a "double-header" (two engines) to take us over the grade.

The pilot of the head engine, because it "punched the wind," I knew would be too cold; so I selected the pilot of the second engine, which was sheltered by the first engine. I stepped on the cowcatcher and found the pilot occupied. In the darkness I felt out the form of a young boy. He was sound asleep. By squeezing, there was room for two on the pilot, and I made the boy hudge over and crawled up beside him. It was a "good" night; the "shacks" (brakemen) didn't bother us, and in no time we were asleep. Once in a while hot cinders or heavy jolts aroused me, when I snuggled closer to the boy and dozed off to the coughing of the engines and the screeching of the wheels.

"Shacks."

The overland made Evanston, Wyoming, and went no farther. A wreck ahead blocked the line. The dead engineer had been brought in, and his body attested the peril of the way. A tramp, also, had been killed, but his body had not been brought in. I talked with the boy. He was thirteen years old. He had run away from his folks in some place in Oregon, and was heading east to his grandmother. He had a tale of cruel treatment in the home he had left that rang true; besides, there was no need for him to lie to me, a nameless hobo on the track.

And that boy was going some, too. He couldn't cover the ground fast enough. When the division superintendents decided to send the overland back over the way it had come, then up on a cross "jerk" to the Oregon Short Line, and back along that road to tap the Union Pacific the other side of the wreck, that boy climbed upon the pilot and said he was going to stay with it. This was too much for the Swede and me. It meant travelling the rest of that frigid night in order to gain no more than a dozen miles or so. We said we'd wait till the wreck was cleared away, and in the meantime get a good sleep.

Now it is no snap to strike a strange town, broke, at midnight, in cold weather, and find a place to sleep. The Swede hadn't a penny. My total assets consisted of two dimes and a nickel. From some of the town boys we learned that beer was five cents, and that the saloons kept open all night. There was our meat. Two glasses of beer would cost ten cents, there would be a stove and chairs, and we could sleep it out till morning. We headed for the lights of a saloon, walking briskly, the snow crunching under our feet, a chill little wind blowing through us.

Alas, I had misunderstood the town boys. Beer was five cents in one saloon only in the whole burg, and we didn't strike that saloon. But the one we entered was all right. A blessed stove was roaring white-hot; there were cosey, cane-bottomed arm-chairs, and a none-too-pleasant-looking barkeeper who glared suspiciously at us as we came in. A man cannot spend continuous days and nights in his clothes, beating trains, fighting soot and cinders, and sleeping anywhere, and maintain a good "front." Our fronts were decidedly against us; but what did we care? I had the price in my jeans.

"Two beers," said I nonchalantly to the barkeeper, and while he drew them, the Swede and I leaned against the bar and yearned secretly for the arm-chairs by the stove.

The barkeeper set the two foaming glasses before us, and with pride I deposited the ten cents. Now I was dead game. As soon as I learned my error in the price I'd have dug up another ten cents. Never mind if it did leave me only a nickel to my name, a stranger in a strange land. I'd have paid it all right. But that barkeeper never gave me a chance. As soon as his eyes spotted the dime I had laid down, he seized the two glasses, one in each hand, and dumped the beer into the sink behind the bar. At the same time, glaring at us malevolently, he said:—

"You've got scabs on your nose. You've got scabs on your nose. You've got scabs on your nose. See!"

I hadn't either, and neither had the Swede. Our noses were all right. The direct bearing of his words was beyond our comprehension, but the indirect bearing was clear as print: he didn't like our looks, and beer was evidently ten cents a glass.

I dug down and laid another dime on the bar, remarking carelessly, "Oh, I thought this was a five-cent joint."

"Your money's no good here," he answered, shoving the two dimes across the bar to me.

Sadly I dropped them back into my pocket, sadly we yearned toward the blessed stove and the arm-chairs, and sadly we went out the door into the frosty night.

But as we went out the door, the barkeeper, still glaring, called after us, "You've got scabs on your nose, see!"

I have seen much of the world since then, journeyed among strange lands and peoples, opened many books, sat in many lecture-halls; but to this day, though I have pondered long and deep, I have been unable to divine the meaning in the cryptic utterance of that barkeeper in Evanston, Wyoming. Our noses *were* all right.

We slept that night over the boilers in an electric-lighting plant. How we discovered that "kipping" place I can't remember. We must have just headed for it, instinctively, as horses head for water or carrier-pigeons head for the home-cote. But it was a night not pleasant to remember. A dozen hoboes were ahead of us on top the boilers, and it was too hot for all of us. To complete our misery, the engineer would not let us stand around down below. He gave us our choice of the boilers or the outside snow.

"You said you wanted to sleep, and so, damn you, sleep," said he to me, when, frantic and beaten out by the heat, I came down into the fire-room.

He pointed out of doors.

"Water," I gasped, wiping the sweat from my eyes, "water."

He pointed out of doors and assured me that down there somewhere in the blackness I'd find the river. I started for the river, got lost in the dark, fell into two or three drifts, gave it up, and returned half-frozen to the top of the boilers. When I had thawed out, I was thirstier than ever. Around me the hoboes were moaning, groaning, sobbing, sighing, gasping, panting, rolling and tossing and floundering heavily in their torment. We were so many lost souls toasting on a griddle in hell, and the engineer, Satan Incarnate, gave us the sole alternative of freezing in the outer cold. The Swede sat up and anathematized passionately the wanderlust in man that sent him tramping and suffering hardships such as that.

"When I get back to Chicago," he perorated, "I'm going to get a job and stick to it till hell freezes over. Then I'll go tramping again."

And, such is the irony of fate, next day, when the wreck ahead was cleared, the Swede and I pulled out of Evanston in the ice-boxes of an "orange special," a fast freight laden with fruit from sunny California. Of course, the ice-boxes were empty on account of the cold weather, but that didn't make them any warmer for us. We entered them through hatchways in the top of the car; the boxes were constructed of galvanized iron, and in that biting weather were not pleasant to the touch. We lay there, shivered and shook, and with chattering teeth held a council wherein we decided that we'd stay by the ice-boxes day and night till we got out of the inhospitable plateau region and down into the Mississippi Valley.

We entered them through hatchways in the top of the car.

But we must eat, and we decided that at the next division we would throw our feet for grub and make a rush back to our ice-boxes. We arrived in the town of Green River late in the afternoon, but too early for supper. Before meal-time is the worst time for "battering" back-doors; but we put on our nerve, swung off the side-ladders as the freight pulled into the yards, and made a run for the houses. We were quickly separated; but we had agreed to meet in the ice-boxes. I had bad luck at first; but in the end, with a couple of "hand-outs" poked into my shirt, I chased for the train. It was pulling out and going fast. The particular refrigerator-car in which we were to meet had already gone by, and half a dozen cars down the train from it I swung on to the side-ladders, went up on top hurriedly, and dropped down into an ice-box.

But a shack had seen me from the caboose, and at the next stop a few miles farther on, Rock Springs, the shack stuck his head into my box and said: "Hit the grit, you son of a toad! Hit the grit!" Also he grabbed me by the heels and dragged me out. I hit the grit all right, and the orange special and the Swede rolled on without me.

Grabbed me by the heels and dragged me out.

Snow was beginning to fall. A cold night was coming on. After dark I hunted around in the railroad yards until I found an empty refrigerator car. In I climbed—not into the ice-boxes, but into the car itself. I swung the heavy doors shut, and their edges, covered with strips of rubber, sealed the car air-tight. The walls were thick. There was no way for the outside cold to get in. But the inside was just as cold as the outside. How to raise the temperature was the problem. But trust a "profesh" for that. Out of my pockets I dug up three or four newspapers. These I burned, one at a time, on the floor of the car. The smoke rose to the top. Not a bit of the heat could escape, and, comfortable and warm, I passed a beautiful night. I didn't wake up once.

In the morning it was still snowing. While throwing my feet for breakfast, I missed an east-bound freight. Later in the day I nailed two other freights and was ditched from both of them. All afternoon no east-bound trains went by. The snow was falling thicker than ever, but at twilight I rode out on the first blind of the overland. As I swung aboard the blind from one side, somebody swung aboard from the other. It was the boy who had run away from Oregon.

Now the first blind of a fast train in a driving snowstorm is no summer picnic. The wind goes right through one, strikes the front of the car, and comes back again. At the first stop, darkness having come on, I went forward and interviewed the fireman. I offered to "shove" coal to the end of his run, which was Rawlins, and my offer was accepted. My work was out on the tender, in the snow, breaking the lumps of coal with a sledge and shovelling it forward to him in the cab. But as I did not have to work all the time, I could come into the cab and warm up now and again.

"Say," I said to the fireman, at my first breathing spell, "there's a little kid back there on the first blind. He's pretty cold."

The cabs on the Union Pacific engines are quite spacious, and we fitted the kid into a warm nook in front of the high seat of the fireman, where the kid promptly fell asleep. We arrived at Rawlins at midnight. The snow was thicker than ever. Here the engine was to go into the round-house, being replaced by a fresh engine. As the train came to a stop, I dropped off the engine steps plump into the arms of a large man in a large overcoat. He began asking me questions, and I promptly demanded who he was. Just as promptly he informed me that he was the sheriff. I drew in my horns and listened and answered.

I offered to "shove" coal to the end of his run.

He began describing the kid who was still asleep in the cab. I did some quick thinking. Evidently the family was on the trail of the kid, and the sheriff had received telegraphed instructions from Oregon. Yes, I had seen the kid. I had met him first in Ogden. The date tallied with the sheriff's information. But the kid was still behind somewhere, I explained, for he had been ditched from that very overland that night when it pulled out of Rock Springs. And all the time I was praying that the kid wouldn't wake up, come down out of the cab, and put the "kibosh" on me.

The sheriff left me in order to interview the shacks, but before he left he said:—

"Bo, this town is no place for you. Understand? You ride this train out, and make no mistake about it. If I catch you after it's gone . . ."

I assured him that it was not through desire that I was in his town; that the only reason I was there was that the train had stopped

It was the sheriff.

there; and that he wouldn't see me for smoke the way I'd get out of his darn town.

While he went to interview the shacks, I jumped back into the cab. The kid was awake and rubbing his eyes. I told him the news and advised him to ride the engine into the round-house. To cut the story short, the kid made the same overland out, riding the pilot, with instructions to make an appeal to the fireman at the first stop for permission to ride in the engine. As for myself, I got ditched. The new fireman was young and not yet lax enough to break the rules of the Company against having tramps in the engine; so he turned down my offer to shove coal. I hope the kid succeeded with him, for all night on the pilot in that blizzard would have meant death.

Strange to say, I do not at this late day remember a detail of how I was ditched at Rawlins. I remember watching the train as it was immediately swallowed up in the snow-storm, and of heading for a saloon to warm up. Here was light and warmth. Everything was in full blast and wide open. Faro, roulette, craps, and poker tables were running, and some mad cowpunchers were making the night merry.[3] I had just succeeded in fraternizing with them and was downing my first drink at their expense, when a heavy hand descended on my shoulder. I looked around and sighed. It was the sheriff.

Without a word he led me out into the snow.

"There's an orange special down there in the yards," said he.

"It's a damn cold night," said I.

"It pulls out in ten minutes," said he.

That was all. There was no discussion. And when that orange special pulled out, I was in the ice-boxes. I thought my feet would freeze before morning, and the last twenty miles into Laramie I stood upright in the hatchway and danced up and down. The snow was too thick for the shacks to see me, and I didn't care if they did.

My quarter of a dollar bought me a hot breakfast at Laramie, and immediately afterward I was on board the blind baggage of an overland that was climbing to the pass through the backbone of the Rockies. One does not ride blind baggages in the daytime; but in this blizzard at the top of the Rocky Mountains I doubted if the shacks would have the heart to put me off. And they didn't. They made a practice of coming forward at every stop to see if I was frozen yet.

At Ames' Monument, at the summit of the Rockies,—I forget the altitude,—the shack came forward for the last time.

"Say, Bo," he said, "you see that freight sidetracked over there to let us go by?"

I saw. It was on the next track, six feet away. A few feet more in that storm and I could not have seen it.

"Well, the 'after-push' of Kelly's Army is in one of them cars. They've got two feet of straw under them, and there's so many of them that they keep the car warm."

His advice was good, and I followed it, prepared, however, if it was a "con game" the shack had given me, to take the blind as the overland pulled out. But it was straight goods. I found the car—a big refrigerator car with the leeward door wide open for ventilation.[4]

I found the car—with the leeward door
open for ventilation.

Up I climbed and in. I stepped on a man's leg, next on some other
man's arm. The light was dim, and all I could make out was arms
and legs and bodies inextricably confused. Never was there such a
tangle of humanity. They were all lying in the straw, and over, and
under, and around one another. Eighty-four husky hoboes take up a
lot of room when they are stretched out. The men I stepped on were
resentful. Their bodies heaved under me like the waves of the sea,
and imparted an involuntary forward movement to me. I could not
find any straw to step upon, so I stepped upon more men. The
resentment increased, so did my forward movement. I lost my footing and sat down with sharp abruptness. Unfortunately, it was on a
man's head. The next moment he had risen on his hands and knees
in wrath, and I was flying through the air. What goes up must come
down, and I came down on another man's head.

What happened after that is very vague in my memory. It was like going through a threshing-machine. I was bandied about from one end of the car to the other. Those eighty-four hoboes winnowed me out till what little was left of me, by some miracle, found a bit of straw to rest upon. I was initiated, and into a jolly crowd. All the rest of that day we rode through the blizzard, and to while the time away it was decided that each man was to tell a story. It was stipulated that each story must be a good one, and, furthermore, that it must be a story no one had ever heard before. The penalty for failure was the threshing-machine. Nobody failed. And I want to say right here that never in my life have I sat at so marvellous a story-telling debauch. Here were eighty-four men from all the world—I made eighty-five; and each man told a masterpiece. It had to be, for it was either masterpiece or threshing-machine.

Late in the afternoon we arrived in Cheyenne. The blizzard was at its height, and though the last meal of all of us had been breakfast, no man cared to throw his feet for supper. All night we rolled on through the storm, and next day found us down on the sweet plains of Nebraska and still rolling. We were out of the storm and the mountains. The blessed sun was shining over a smiling land, and we had eaten nothing for twenty-four hours. We found out that the freight would arrive about noon at a town, if I remember right, that was called Grand Island.

We took up a collection and sent a telegram to the authorities of that town. The text of the message was that eighty-five healthy, hungry hoboes would arrive about noon and that it would be a good idea to have dinner ready for them. The authorities of Grand Island had two courses open to them. They could feed us, or they could throw us in jail. In the latter event they'd have to feed us anyway, and they decided wisely that one meal would be the cheaper way.

When the freight rolled into Grand Island at noon, we were sitting on the tops of the cars and dangling our legs in the sunshine. All the police in the burg were on the reception committee. They marched us in squads to the various hotels and restaurants, where dinners were spread for us. We had been thirty-six hours without food, and we didn't have to be taught what to do. After that we were marched back to the railroad station. The police had thoughtfully compelled the freight to wait for us. She pulled out slowly, and the eighty-five of us, strung out along the track, swarmed up the side-ladders. We "captured" the train.

We had no supper that evening—at least the "push" didn't, but I did. Just at supper time, as the freight was pulling out of a small town, a man climbed into the car where I was playing pedro with three other stiffs.[5] The man's shirt was bulging suspiciously. In his hand he carried a battered quart-measure from which arose steam. I smelled "Java." I turned my cards over to one of the stiffs who was looking on, and excused myself. Then, in the other end of the car, pursued by envious glances, we sat down with the man who had climbed aboard and shared his "Java" and the handouts that had bulged his shirt. It was the Swede.

At about ten o'clock in the evening, we arrived at Omaha.

"Let's shake the push," said the Swede to me.

"Sure," said I.

As the freight pulled into Omaha, we made ready to do so. But the people of Omaha were also ready. The Swede and I hung upon the side-ladders, ready to drop off. But the freight did not stop. Furthermore, long rows of policemen, their brass buttons and stars glittering in the electric lights, were lined up on each side of the track. The Swede and I knew what would happen to us if we ever dropped off into their arms. We stuck by the side-ladders, and the train rolled on across the Missouri River to Council Bluffs.

"General" Kelly, with an army of two thousand hoboes, lay in camp at Chautauqua Park, several miles away. The after-push we were with was General Kelly's rearguard, and, detraining at Council Bluffs, it started to march to camp. The night had turned cold, and heavy wind-squalls, accompanied by rain, were chilling and wetting us. Many police were guarding us and herding us to the camp. The Swede and I watched our chance and made a successful get-away.

The rain began coming down in torrents, and in the darkness, unable to see our hands in front of our faces, like a pair of blind men we fumbled about for shelter. Our instinct served us, for in no time we stumbled upon a saloon—not a saloon that was open and doing business, not merely a saloon that was closed for the night, and not even a saloon with a permanent address, but a saloon propped up on big timbers, with rollers underneath, that was being moved from somewhere to somewhere. The doors were locked. A squall of wind and rain drove down upon us. We did not hesitate. Smash went the door, and in we went.

I have made some tough camps in my time, "carried the banner" in infernal metropolises, bedded in pools of water, slept in the snow under two blankets when the spirit thermometer registered seventy-four degrees below zero (which is a mere trifle of one hundred and six degrees of frost); but I want to say right here that never did I make a tougher camp, pass a more miserable night, than that night I passed with the Swede in the itinerant saloon at Council Bluffs.[6] In the first place, the building, perched up as it was in the air, had exposed a multitude of openings in the floor through which the wind whistled. In the second place, the bar was empty; there was no bottled fire-water with which we could warm ourselves and forget our misery. We had no blankets, and in our wet clothes, wet to the skin, we tried to sleep. I rolled under the bar, and the Swede rolled under the table. The holes and crevices in the floor made it impossible, and at the end of half an hour I crawled up on top the bar. A little later the Swede crawled up on top his table.

And there we shivered and prayed for daylight. I know, for one, that I shivered until I could shiver no more, till the shivering muscles exhausted themselves and merely ached horribly. The Swede moaned and groaned, and every little while, through chattering teeth, he muttered, "Never again; never again." He muttered this phrase repeatedly, ceaselessly, a thousand times; and when he dozed, he went on muttering it in his sleep.

At the first gray of dawn we left our house of pain, and outside, found ourselves in a mist, dense and chill. We stumbled on till we came to the railroad track. I was going back to Omaha to throw my feet for breakfast; my companion was going on to Chicago. The moment for parting had come. Our palsied hands went out to each other. We were both shivering. When we tried to speak, our teeth chattered us back into silence. We stood alone, shut off from the world; all that we could see was a short length of railroad track, both ends of which were lost in the driving mist. We stared dumbly at each other, our clasped hands shaking sympathetically. The Swede's face was blue with the cold, and I know mine must have been.

"Never again what?" I managed to articulate.

Speech strove for utterance in the Swede's throat; then, faint and distant, in a thin whisper from the very bottom of his frozen soul, came the words:—

"Never again a hobo."

He paused, and, as he went on again, his voice gathered strength and huskiness as it affirmed his will.

"Never again a hobo. I'm going to get a job. You'd better do the same. Nights like this make rheumatism."

He wrung my hand.

"Good-by, Bo," said he.

"Good-by, Bo," said I.

The next we were swallowed up from each other by the mist. It was our final passing. But here's to you, Mr. Swede, wherever you are. I hope you got that job.

ROAD-KIDS AND GAY-CATS

Every once in a while, in newspapers, magazines, and biographical dictionaries, I run upon sketches of my life, wherein, delicately phrased, I learn that it was in order to study sociology that I became a tramp. This is very nice and thoughtful of the biographers, but it is inaccurate. I became a tramp—well, because of the life that was in me, of the wanderlust in my blood that would not let me rest. Sociology was merely incidental; it came afterward, in the same manner that a wet skin follows a ducking. I went on "The Road" because I couldn't keep away from it; because I hadn't the price of the railroad fare in my jeans; because I was so made that I couldn't work all my life on "one same shift"; because—well, just because it was easier to than not to.

It happened in my own town, in Oakland, when I was sixteen. At that time I had attained a dizzy reputation in my chosen circle of adventurers, by whom I was known as the Prince of the Oyster Pirates. It is true, those immediately outside my circle, such as honest bay-sailors, longshoremen, yachtsmen, and the legal owners of the oysters, called me "tough," "hoodlum," "smoudge," "thief," "robber," and various other not nice things—all of which was complimentary and but served to increase the dizziness of the high place in which I sat. At that time I had not read "Paradise Lost," and later, when I read Milton's "Better to reign in hell than serve in heaven," I was fully convinced that great minds run in the same channels.[1]

It was at this time that the fortuitous concatenation of events sent me upon my first adventure on The Road. It happened that there was nothing doing in oysters just then; that at Benicia, forty miles away, I had some blankets I wanted to get; and that at Port Costa, several miles from Benicia, a stolen boat lay at anchor in charge of the constable. Now this boat was owned by a friend of mine, by name Dinny McCrea. It had been stolen and left at Port Costa by Whiskey Bob, another friend of mine. (Poor Whiskey Bob! Only last winter his body was picked up on the beach shot full of holes by nobody knows whom.) I had come down from "up river" some time before, and reported to Dinny McCrea the whereabouts of his boat; and Dinny McCrea had promptly offered ten dollars to me if I should bring it down to Oakland to him.

Time was heavy on my hands. I sat on the dock and talked it over with Nickey the Greek, another idle oyster pirate. "Let's go," said I, and Nickey was willing. He was "broke." I possessed fifty cents and a small skiff. The former I invested and loaded into the latter in the form of crackers, canned corned beef, and a ten-cent bottle of French mustard. (We were keen on French mustard in those days.) Then, late in the afternoon, we hoisted our small spritsail and started. We sailed all night, and next morning, on the first of a glorious flood-tide, a fair wind behind us, we came booming up the Carquinez Straits to Port Costa. There lay the stolen boat, not twenty-five feet from the wharf. We ran alongside and doused our little spritsail. I sent Nickey forward to lift the anchor, while I began casting off the gaskets.

A man ran out on the wharf and hailed us. It was the constable. It suddenly came to me that I had neglected to get a written authorization from Dinny McCrea to take possession of his boat. Also, I knew that constable wanted to charge at least twenty-five dollars in fees for capturing the boat from Whiskey Bob and subsequently taking care of it. And my last fifty cents had been blown in for corned beef and French mustard, and the reward was only ten dollars anyway. I shot a glance forward to Nickey. He had the anchor up-and-down and was straining at it. "Break her out," I whispered to him, and turned and shouted back to the constable. The result was that he and I were talking at the same time, our spoken thoughts colliding in mid-air and making gibberish.

The constable grew more imperative, and perforce I had to listen. Nickey was heaving on the anchor till I thought he'd burst a blood-vessel. When the constable got done with his threats and warnings, I asked him who he was. The time he lost in telling me enabled Nickey to break out the anchor. I was doing some quick calculating. At the feet of the constable a ladder ran down the dock to the water, and to the ladder was moored a skiff. The oars were in it. But it was padlocked. I gambled everything on that padlock. I felt the breeze on my cheek, saw the surge of the tide, looked at the remaining gaskets that confined the sail, ran my eyes up the halyards to the blocks and knew that all was clear, and then threw off all dissimulation.[2]

"In with her!" I shouted to Nickey, and sprang to the gaskets, casting them loose and thanking my stars that Whiskey Bob had tied them in square-knots instead of "grannies."

The constable had slid down the ladder and was fumbling with a key at the padlock. The anchor came aboard and the last gasket was loosed at the same instant that the constable freed the skiff and jumped to the oars.

"Peak-halyards!" I commanded my crew, at the same time swinging on to the throat-halyards. Up came the sail on the run. I belayed and ran aft to the tiller.[3]

"Stretch her!" I shouted to Nickey at the peak. The constable was just reaching for our stern. A puff of wind caught us, and we shot away. It was great. If I'd had a black flag, I know I'd have run it up in triumph. The constable stood up in the skiff, and paled the glory of the day with the vividness of his language. Also, he wailed for a gun. You see, that was another gamble we had taken.

Anyway, we weren't stealing the boat. It wasn't the constable's. We were merely stealing his fees, which was his particular form of graft. And we weren't stealing the fees for ourselves, either; we were stealing them for my friend, Dinny McCrea.

Benicia was made in a few minutes, and a few minutes later my blankets were aboard. I shifted the boat down to the far end of Steamboat Wharf, from which point of vantage we could see anybody coming after us. There was no telling. Maybe the Port Costa constable would telephone to the Benicia constable. Nickey and I held a council of war. We lay on deck in the warm sun, the fresh breeze on our checks, the flood-tide rippling and swirling past. It was impossible to start back to Oakland till afternoon, when the ebb

A puff of wind caught us, and we shot away.

would begin to run. But we figured that the constable would have an eye out on the Carquinez Straits when the ebb started, and that nothing remained for us but to wait for the following ebb, at two o'clock next morning, when we could slip by Cerberus in the darkness.

So we lay on deck, smoked cigarettes, and were glad that we were alive. I spat over the side and gauged the speed of the current.

"With this wind, we could run this flood clear to Rio Vista," I said.

"And it's fruit-time on the river," said Nickey.

"And low water on the river," said I. "It's the best time of the year to make Sacramento."

We sat up and looked at each other. The glorious west wind was pouring over us like wine. We both spat over the side and gauged the current. Now I contend that it was all the fault of that flood-tide and fair wind. They appealed to our sailor instinct. If it had not been for them, the whole chain of events that was to put me upon The Road would have broken down.

We said no word, but cast off our moorings and hoisted sail. Our adventures up the Sacramento River are no part of this narrative. We subsequently made the city of Sacramento and tied up at a wharf. The water was fine, and we spent most of our time in swimming. On the sand-bar above the railroad bridge we fell in with a bunch of boys likewise in swimming. Between swims we lay on the bank and talked. They talked differently from the fellows I had been used to herding with. It was a new vernacular. They were road-kids, and with every word they uttered the lure of The Road laid hold of me more imperiously.

"When I was down in Alabama," one kid would begin; or, another, "Coming up on the C. & A. from K.C."; whereat, a third kid, "On the C. & A. there ain't no steps to the 'blinds.'" And I would lie silently in the sand and listen. "It was at a little town in Ohio on the Lake Shore and Michigan Southern," a kid would start; and another, "Ever ride the Cannonball on the Wabash?"; and yet another, "Nope, but I've been on the White Mail out of Chicago." "Talk about rail-roadin'—wait till you hit the Pennsylvania, four tracks, no water tanks, take water on the fly, that's goin' some." "The Northern Pacific's a bad road now." "Salinas is on the 'hog,' the 'bulls' is 'horstile.'" "I got 'pinched' at El Paso, along with Moke Kid." "Talkin' of 'poke-outs,' wait till you hit the French country out of Montreal—not a word of English—you say, '*Mongee, Madame, mongee, no spika da French*,' an' rub your stomach an' look hungry, an' she gives you a slice of sow-belly an' a chunk of dry 'punk.'"

And I continued to lie in the sand and listen. These wanderers made my oyster-piracy look like thirty cents. A new world was calling to me in every word that was spoken—a world of rods and gunnels, blind baggages and "side-door Pullmans," "bulls" and "shacks," "floppings" and "chewin's," "pinches" and "get-aways," "strong arms" and "bindle-stiffs," "punks" and "profesh." And it all spelled Adventure. Very well; I would tackle this new world. I "lined" myself up alongside those road-kids. I was just as strong as any of them, just as quick, just as nervy, and my brain was just as good.

After the swim, as evening came on, they dressed and went up town. I went along. The kids began "battering" the "main-stem" for "light pieces," or, in other words, begging for money on the main street. I had never begged in my life, and this was the hardest thing for me to stomach when I first went on The Road. I had absurd notions about begging. My philosophy, up to that time, was that it was finer to steal than to beg; and that robbery was finer still because the risk and the penalty were proportionately greater. As an oyster pirate I had already earned convictions at the hands of justice, which, if I had tried to serve them, would have required a thousand years in state's prison. To rob was manly; to beg was sordid and despicable. But I developed in the days to come all right, all right, till I came to look upon begging as a joyous prank, a game of wits, a nerve-exerciser.

That first night, however, I couldn't rise to it; and the result was that when the kids were ready to go to a restaurant and eat, I wasn't. I was broke. Meeny Kid, I think it was, gave me the price, and we all ate together. But while I ate, I meditated. The receiver, it was said, was as bad as the thief; Meeny Kid had done the begging, and I was profiting by it. I decided that the receiver was a whole lot worse than the thief, and that it shouldn't happen again. And it didn't. I turned out next day and threw my feet as well as the next one.

Nickey the Greek's ambition didn't run to The Road. He was not a success at throwing his feet, and he stowed away one night on a barge and went down river to San Francisco. I met him, only a week ago, at a pugilistic carnival. He has progressed. He sat in a place of honor at the ring-side. He is now a manager of prize-fighters and proud of it. In fact, in a small way, in local sportdom, he is quite a shining light.

"No kid is a road-kid until he has gone over 'the hill' "—such was the law of The Road I heard expounded in Sacramento. All right, I'd go over the hill and matriculate. "The hill," by the way, was the Sierra Nevadas. The whole gang was going over the hill on a jaunt, and of course I'd go along. It was French Kid's first adventure on The Road. He had just run away from his people in San Francisco. It was up to him and me to deliver the goods. In passing, I may remark that my old title of "Prince" had vanished. I had received my "monica." I was now "Sailor Kid," later to be known as "Frisco Kid," when I had put the Rockies between me and my native state.

At 10.20 P.M. the Central Pacific overland pulled out of the depot at Sacramento for the East—that particular item of time-table is indelibly engraved on my memory. There were about a dozen in our gang, and we strung out in the darkness ahead of the train ready to take her out. All the local road-kids that we knew came down to see us off—also, to "ditch" us if they could. That was their idea of a joke, and there were only about forty of them to carry it out. Their ringleader was a crackerjack road-kid named Bob. Sacramento was his home town, but he'd hit The Road pretty well everywhere over the whole country. He took French Kid and me aside and gave us advice something like this: "We're goin' to try an' ditch your bunch, see? Youse two are weak. The rest of the push can take care of itself. So, as soon as youse two nail a blind, deck her. An' stay on the decks till youse pass Roseville Junction, at which burg the constables are horstile, sloughin' in everybody on sight."

The engine whistled and the overland pulled out. There were three blinds on her—room for all of us. The dozen of us who were trying to make her out would have preferred to slip aboard quietly; but our forty friends crowded on with the most amazing and shameless publicity and advertisement. Following Bob's advice, I immediately "decked her," that is, climbed up on top of the roof of one of the mail-cars. There I lay down, my heart jumping a few extra beats, and listened to the fun. The whole train crew was forward, and the ditching went on fast and furious. After the train had run half a mile, it stopped, and the crew came forward again and ditched the survivors. I, alone, had made the train out.

Back at the depot, about him two or three of the push that had witnessed the accident, lay French Kid with both legs off. French Kid had slipped or stumbled—that was all, and the wheels had done the rest. Such was my initiation to The Road. It was two years afterward when I next saw French Kid and examined his "stumps." This was an act of courtesy. "Cripples" always like to have their stumps examined. One of the entertaining sights on The Road is to witness the meeting of two cripples. Their common disability is a fruitful source of conversation; and they tell how it happened, describe what they know of the amputation, pass critical judgment on their own and each other's surgeons, and wind up by withdrawing to one side, taking off bandages and wrappings, and comparing stumps.

But it was not until several days later, over in Nevada, when the push caught up with me, that I learned of French Kid's accident. The push itself arrived in bad condition. It had gone through a train-wreck in the snow-sheds; Happy Joe was on crutches with two mashed legs, and the rest were nursing skins and bruises.

In the meantime, I lay on the roof of the mail-car, trying to remember whether Roseville Junction, against which burg Bob had warned me, was the first stop or the second stop. To make sure, I delayed descending to the platform of the blind until after the second stop. And then I didn't descend. I was new to the game, and I felt safer where I was. But I never told the push that I held down the decks the whole night, clear across the Sierras, through snow-sheds and tunnels, and down to Truckee on the other side, where I arrived at seven in the morning. Such a thing was disgraceful, and I'd have been a common laughing-stock. This is the first time I have confessed the truth about that first ride over the hill. As for the push, it decided that I was all right, and when I came back over the hill to Sacramento, I was a full-fledged road-kid.

Yet I had much to learn. Bob was my mentor, and he was all right. I remember one evening (it was fair-time in Sacramento, and we were knocking about and having a good time) when I lost my hat in a fight. There was I bare-headed in the street, and it was Bob to the rescue. He took me to one side from the push and told me what to do. I was a bit timid of his advice. I had just come out of jail, where I had been three days, and I knew that if the police "pinched" me again, I'd get good and "soaked." On the other hand, I couldn't show the white feather. I'd been over the hill, I was running full-fledged with the push, and it was up to me to deliver the goods. So I accepted Bob's advice, and he came along with me to see that I did it up brown.

We took our position on K Street, on the corner, I think, of Fifth. It was early in the evening and the street was crowded. Bob studied the head-gear of every Chinaman that passed. I used to wonder how the road-kids all managed to wear "five-dollar Stetson stiff-rims," and now I knew. They got them, the way I was going to get mine, from the Chinese. I was nervous—there were so many people about;

There was I bare-headed in the street.

but Bob was cool as an iceberg. Several times, when I started forward toward a Chinaman, all nerved and keyed up, Bob dragged me back. He wanted me to get a good hat, and one that fitted. Now a hat came by that was the right size but not new; and, after a dozen impossible hats, along would come one that was new but not the right size. And when one did come by that was new and the right size, the rim was too large or not large enough. My, Bob was finicky. I was so wrought up that I'd have snatched any kind of a head-covering.

At last came the hat, the one hat in Sacramento for me. I knew it was a winner as soon as I looked at it. I glanced at Bob. He sent a sweeping look-about for police, then nodded his head. I lifted the hat from the Chinaman's head and pulled it down on my own. It was a perfect fit. Then I started. I heard Bob crying out, and I caught a glimpse of him blocking the irate Mongolian and tripping him up. I ran on. I turned up the next corner, and around the next. This street was not so crowded as K, and I walked along in quietude, catching my breath and congratulating myself upon my hat and my get-away.

And then, suddenly, around the corner at my back, came the bare-headed Chinaman. With him were a couple more Chinamen, and at their heels were half a dozen men and boys. I sprinted to the next corner, crossed the street, and rounded the following corner. I decided that I had surely played him out, and I dropped into a walk again. But around the corner at my heels came that persistent Mongolian. It was the old story of the hare and the tortoise. He could not run so fast as I, but he stayed with it, plodding along at a shambling and deceptive trot, and wasting much good breath in noisy imprecations. He called all Sacramento to witness the dishonor that had been done him, and a goodly portion of Sacramento heard and flocked at his heels. And I ran on like the hare, and ever that persistent Mongolian, with the increasing rabble, overhauled me. But finally, when a policeman had joined his following, I let out all my links. I twisted and turned, and I swear I ran at least twenty blocks on the straight away. And I never saw that Chinaman again. The hat was a dandy, a brand-new Stetson, just out of the shop, and it was the envy of the whole push. Furthermore, it was the symbol that I had delivered the goods. I wore it for over a year.

Road-kids are nice little chaps—when you get them alone and they are telling you "how it happened"; but take my word for it, watch out for them when they run in pack. Then they are wolves, and like wolves they are capable of dragging down the strongest man. At such times they are not cowardly. They will fling themselves upon a man and hold on with every ounce of strength in their wiry bodies, till he is thrown and helpless. More than once have I seen them do it, and I know whereof I speak. Their motive is usually robbery. And watch out for the "strong arm." Every kid in the push I travelled with was expert at it. Even French Kid mastered it before he lost his legs.

I have strong upon me now a vision of what I once saw in "The Willows." The Willows was a clump of trees in a waste piece of land near the railway depot and not more than five minutes walk from the heart of Sacramento. It is night-time, and the scene is illumined by the thin light of stars. I see a husky laborer in the midst of a pack of road-kids. He is infuriated and cursing them, not a bit afraid, confident of his own strength. He weighs about one hundred and eighty pounds, and his muscles are hard; but he doesn't know what he is up against. The kids are snarling. It is not pretty. They make a rush from all sides, and he lashes out and whirls. Barber Kid is standing beside me. As the man whirls, Barber Kid leaps forward and does the trick. Into the man's back goes his knee; around the man's neck, from behind, passes his right hand, the bone of the wrist pressing against the jugular vein. Barber Kid throws his whole weight backward. It is a powerful leverage. Besides, the man's wind has been shut off. It is the strong arm.

The man resists, but he is already practically helpless. The road-kids are upon him from every side, clinging to arms and legs and body, and like a wolf at the throat of a moose Barber Kid hangs on and drags backward. Over the man goes, and down under the heap. Barber Kid changes the position of his own body, but never lets go. While some of the kids are "going through" the victim, others are holding his legs so that he cannot kick and thresh about. They improve the opportunity by taking off the man's shoes. As for him, he has given in. He is beaten. Also, what of the strong arm at his throat, he is short of wind. He is making ugly choking noises, and the kids hurry. They really don't want to kill him. All is done. At a word all holds are released at once, and the kids scatter, one of them lugging the shoes—he knows where he can get half a dollar for them. The man sits up and looks about him, dazed and helpless. Even if he wanted to, bare-footed pursuit in the darkness would be hopeless. I linger a moment and watch him. He is feeling at his throat, making dry, hawking noises, and jerking his head in a quaint way as though to assure himself that the neck is not dislocated. Then I slip away to join the push, and see that man no more—though I shall always see him, sitting there in the starlight, somewhat dazed, a bit frightened, greatly dishevelled, and making quaint jerking movements of head and neck.

Drunken men are the especial prey of the road-kids. Robbing a drunken man they call "rolling a stiff"; and wherever they are, they are on the constant lookout for drunks. The drunk is their particular meat, as the fly is the particular meat of the spider. The rolling of a stiff is ofttimes an amusing sight, especially when the stiff is helpless and when interference is unlikely. At the first swoop the stiff's money and jewellery go. Then the kids sit around their victim in a sort of pow-wow. A kid generates a fancy for the stiff's necktie. Off it comes. Another kid is after underclothes. Off they come, and a knife quickly abbreviates arms and legs. Friendly hoboes may be called in to take the coat and trousers, which are too large for the kids. And in the end they depart, leaving beside the stiff the heap of their discarded rags.

Drunken men are the especial prey of the road-kids.

Another vision comes to me. It is a dark night. My push is coming along the sidewalk in the suburbs. Ahead of us, under an electric light, a man crosses the street diagonally. There is something tentative and desultory in his walk. The kids scent the game on the instant. The man is drunk. He blunders across the opposite sidewalk and is lost in the darkness as he takes a short-cut through a vacant lot. No hunting cry is raised, but the pack flings itself forward in quick pursuit. In the middle of the vacant lot it comes upon him. But what is this?—snarling and strange forms, small and dim and menacing, are between the pack and its prey. It is another pack of road-kids, and in the hostile pause we learn that it is their meat, that they have been trailing it a dozen blocks and more and that we are butting in. But it is the world primeval. These wolves are baby wolves. (As a matter of fact, I don't think one of them was over twelve or thirteen years of age. I met some of them afterward, and learned that they had just arrived that day over the hill, and that they hailed from Denver and Salt Lake City.) Our pack flings forward. The baby wolves squeal and screech and fight like little demons. All about the drunken man rages the struggle for the possession of him. Down he goes in the thick of it, and the combat rages over his body after the fashion of the Greeks and Trojans over the body and armor of a fallen hero. Amid cries and tears and wailings the baby wolves are dispossessed, and my pack rolls the stiff. But always I remember the poor stiff and his befuddled amazement at the abrupt eruption of battle in the vacant lot. I see him now, dim in the darkness, titubating in stupid wonder, good-naturedly essaying the rôle of peacemaker in that multitudinous scrap the significance of which he did not understand, and the really hurt expression on his face when he, unoffending he, was clutched at by many hands and dragged down in the thick of the press.

"Bindle-stiffs" are favorite prey of the road-kids. A bindle-stiff is a working tramp. He takes his name from the roll of blankets he carries, which is known as a "bindle." Because he does work, a bindle-stiff is expected usually to have some small change about him, and it is after that small change that the road-kids go. The best hunting-ground for bindle-stiffs is in the sheds, barns, lumber-yards, railroad-yards, etc., on the edges of a city, and the time for hunting is the night, when the bindle-stiff seeks these places to roll up in his blankets and sleep.

"Gay-cats" also come to grief at the hands of the road-kids. In more familiar parlance, gay-cats are short-horns, *chechaquos,* new chums, or tenderfeet. A gay-cat is a newcomer on The Road who is man-grown, or, at least, youth-grown. A boy on The Road, on the other hand, no matter how green he is, is never a gay-cat; he is a road-kid or a "punk," and if he travels with a "profesh," he is known possessively as a "prushun." I was never a prushun, for I did not take kindly to possession. I was first a road-kid and then a profesh. Because I started in young, I practically skipped my gay-cat apprenticeship. For a short period, during the time I was exchanging my 'Frisco Kid monica for that of Sailor Jack, I labored under the suspicion of being a gay-cat. But closer acquaintance on the part of those that suspected me quickly disabused their minds, and in a short time I acquired the unmistakable airs and ear-marks of the blowed-in-the-glass profesh. And be it known, here and now, that the profesh are the aristocracy of The Road. They are the lords and masters, the aggressive men, the primordial noblemen, the *blond beasts* so beloved of Nietzsche.

When I came back over the hill from Nevada, I found that some river pirate had stolen Dinny McCrea's boat. (A funny thing at this day is that I cannot remember what became of the skiff in which Nickey the Greek and I sailed from Oakland to Port Costa. I know that the constable didn't get it, and I know that it didn't go with us up the Sacramento River, and that is all I do know.) With the loss of Dinny McCrea's boat, I was pledged to The Road; and when I grew tired of Sacramento, I said good-by to the push (which, in its friendly way, tried to ditch me from a freight as I left town) and started on a *passear* down the valley of the San Joaquin.[4] The Road had gripped me and would not let me go; and later, when I had voyaged to sea and done one thing and another, I returned to The Road to make longer flights, to be a "comet" and a profesh, and to plump into the bath of sociology that wet me to the skin.

TWO THOUSAND STIFFS

A "stiff" is a tramp. It was once my fortune to travel a few weeks with a "push" that numbered two thousand. This was known as "Kelly's Army." Across the wild and woolly West, clear from California, General Kelly and his heroes had captured trains; but they fell down when they crossed the Missouri and went up against the effete East. The East hadn't the slightest intention of giving free transportation to two thousand hoboes. Kelly's Army lay helplessly for some time at Council Bluffs. The day I joined it, made desperate by delay, it marched out to capture a train.

It was quite an imposing sight. General Kelly sat a magnificent black charger, and with waving banners, to the martial music of fife and drum corps, company by company, in two divisions, his two thousand stiffs countermarched before him and hit the wagon-road to the little burg of Weston, seven miles away. Being the latest recruit, I was in the last company, of the last regiment, of the Second Division, and, furthermore, in the last rank of the rear-guard. The army went into camp at Weston beside the railroad track—beside the tracks, rather, for two roads went through: the Chicago, Milwaukee, and St. Paul, and the Rock Island.

Our intention was to take the first train out, but the railroad officials "coppered" our play—and won. There was no first train. They tied up the two lines and stopped running trains. In the meantime, while we lay by the dead tracks, the good people of Omaha and Council Bluffs were bestirring themselves. Preparations were making to form a mob, capture a train in Council Bluffs, run it down to us, and make us a present of it. The railroad officials coppered that play, too. They didn't wait for the mob. Early in the morning of the second day, an engine, with a single private car attached, arrived at the station and side-tracked. At this sign that life had renewed in the dead roads, the whole army lined up beside the track.

But never did life renew so monstrously on a dead railroad as it did on those two roads. From the west came the whistle of a locomotive. It was coming in our direction, bound east. We were bound east. A stir of preparation ran down our ranks. The whistle tooted fast and furiously, and the train thundered at top speed. The hobo didn't live that could have boarded it. Another locomotive whistled, and another train came through at top speed, and another, and another, train after train, train after train, till toward the last the trains were composed of passenger coaches, box-cars, flat-cars, dead engines, cabooses, mailcars, wrecking appliances, and all the riff-raff of worn-out and abandoned rolling-stock that collects in the yards of great railways. When the yards at Council Bluffs had been completely cleaned, the private car and engine went east, and the tracks died for keeps.

That day went by, and the next, and nothing moved, and in the meantime, pelted by sleet, and rain, and hail, the two thousand hoboes lay beside the track. But that night the good people of Council Bluffs went the railroad officials one better. A mob formed in Council Bluffs, crossed the river to Omaha, and there joined with another mob in a raid on the Union Pacific yards. First they captured an engine, next they knocked a train together, and then the united mobs piled aboard, crossed the Missouri, and ran down the Rock Island right of way to turn the train over to us. The railway officials tried to copper this play, but fell down, to the mortal terror of the section boss and one member of the section gang at Weston. This pair, under secret telegraphic orders, tried to wreck our train-load of sympathizers by tearing up the track. It happened that we were suspicious and had our patrols out. Caught red-handed at train-wrecking, and surrounded by twenty hundred infuriated hoboes, that section-gang boss and assistant prepared to meet death. I don't remember what saved them, unless it was the arrival of the train.

It was our turn to fall down, and we did, hard. In their haste, the two mobs had neglected to make up a sufficiently long train. There wasn't room for two thousand hoboes to ride. So the mobs and the hoboes had a talkfest, fraternized, sang songs, and parted, the mobs going back on their captured train to Omaha, the hoboes pulling out next morning on a hundred-and-forty-mile march to Des Moines. It was not until Kelly's Army crossed the Missouri that it began to walk, and after that it never rode again. It cost the railroads slathers of money, but they were acting on principle, and they won.

Underwood, Leola, Menden, Avoca, Walnut, Marno, Atlantic, Wyoto, Anita, Adair, Adam, Casey, Stuart, Dexter, Carlham, De Soto, Van Meter, Booneville, Commerce, Valley Junction—how the names of the towns come back to me as I con the map and trace our route through the fat Iowa Country! And the hospitable Iowa farmer-folk! They turned out with their wagons and carried our baggage; gave us hot lunches at noon by the wayside; mayors of comfortable little towns made speeches of welcome and hastened us on our way; deputations of little girls and maidens came out to meet us, and the good citizens turned out by hundreds, locked arms, and marched with us down their main streets. It was circus day when we came to town, and every day was circus day, for there were many towns.

In the evenings our camps were invaded by whole populations. Every company had its campfire, and around each fire something was doing. The cooks in my company, Company L, were song-and-dance artists and contributed most of our entertainment. In another part of the encampment the glee club would be singing—one of its star voices was the "Dentist," drawn from Company L, and we were mighty proud of him. Also, he pulled teeth for the whole army, and, since the extractions usually occurred at meal-time, our digestions were stimulated by variety of incident. The Dentist had no anæsthetics, but two or three of us were always on tap to volunteer to hold down the patient. In addition to the stunts of the companies and the glee club, church services were usually held, local preachers officiating, and always there was a great making of political speeches. All these things ran neck and neck; it was a full-blown Midway. A lot of talent can be dug out of two thousand hoboes. I remember we had a picked baseball nine, and on Sundays we made a practice of putting it all over the local nines. Sometimes we did it twice on Sundays.

Last year, while on a lecturing trip, I rode into Des Moines in a Pullman—I don't mean a "side-door Pullman," but the real thing. On the outskirts of the city I saw the old stove-works, and my heart leaped. It was there, at the stove-works, a dozen years before, that the Army lay down and swore a mighty oath that its feet were sore and that it would walk no more. We took possession of the stove-works and told Des Moines that we had come to stay—that we'd walked in, but we'd be blessed if we'd walk out. Des Moines was hospitable, but this was too much of a good thing. Do a little mental arithmetic, gentle reader. Two thousand hoboes, eating three square meals, make six thousand meals per day, forty-two thousand meals per week, or one hundred and sixty-eight thousand meals per shortest month in the calendar. That's going some. We had no money. It was up to Des Moines.

Des Moines was desperate. We lay in camp, made political speeches, held sacred concerts, pulled teeth, played baseball and seven-up, and ate our six thousand meals per day, and Des Moines paid for it. Des Moines pleaded with the railroads, but they were obdurate; they had said we shouldn't ride, and that settled it. To permit us to ride would be to establish a precedent, and there weren't going to be any precedents. And still we went on eating. That was the terrifying factor in the situation. We were bound for Washington, and Des Moines would have had to float municipal bonds to pay all our railroad fares, even at special rates, and if we remained much longer, she'd have to float bonds anyway to feed us.

Then some local genius solved the problem. We wouldn't walk. Very good. We should ride. From Des Moines to Keokuk on the Mississippi flowed the Des Moines River. This particular stretch of river was three hundred miles long. We could ride on it, said the local genius; and, once equipped with floating stock, we could ride on down the Mississippi to the Ohio, and thence up the Ohio, winding up with a short portage over the mountains to Washington.

Des Moines took up a subscription. Public-spirited citizens contributed several thousand dollars. Lumber, rope, nails, and cotton for calking were bought in large quantities, and on the banks of the Des Moines was inaugurated a tremendous era of shipbuilding.

Now the Des Moines is a picayune stream, unduly dignified by the appellation of "river." In our spacious western land it would be called a "creek." The oldest inhabitants shook their heads and said we couldn't make it, that there wasn't enough water to float us. Des Moines didn't care, so long as it got rid of us, and we were such well-fed optimists that we didn't care either.

On Wednesday, May 9, 1894, we got under way and started on our colossal picnic. Des Moines had got off pretty easily, and she certainly owes a statue in bronze to the local genius who got her out of her difficulty. True, Des Moines had to pay for our boats; we had eaten sixty-six thousand meals at the stove-works; and we took twelve thousand additional meals along with us in our commissary—as a precaution against famine in the wilds; but then, think what it would have meant if we had remained at Des Moines eleven months instead of eleven days. Also, when we departed, we promised Des Moines we'd come back if the river failed to float us.

It was all very well having twelve thousand meals in the commissary, and no doubt the commissary "ducks" enjoyed them; for the commissary promptly got lost, and my boat, for one, never saw it again. The company formation was hopelessly broken up during the river-trip. In any camp of men there will always be found a certain percentage of shirks, of helpless, of just ordinary, and of hustlers. There were ten men in my boat, and they were the cream of Company L. Every man was a hustler. For two reasons I was included in the ten. First, I was as good a hustler as ever "threw his feet," and next, I was "Sailor Jack." I understood boats and boating. The ten of us forgot the remaining forty men of Company L, and by the time we had missed one meal we promptly forgot the commissary. We were independent. We went down the river "on our own," hustling our "chewin's," beating every boat in the fleet, and, alas that I must say it, sometimes taking possession of the stores the farmer-folk had collected for the Army.

For a good part of the three hundred miles we were from half a day to a day or so in advance of the Army. We had managed to get hold of several American flags. When we approached a small town, or when we saw a group of farmers gathered on the bank, we ran up our flags, called ourselves the "advance boat," and demanded to know what provisions had been collected for the Army. We represented the Army, of course, and the provisions were turned over to us. But there wasn't anything small about us. We never took more than we could get away with. But we did take the cream of everything. For instance, if some philanthropic farmer had donated several dollars' worth of tobacco, we took it. So, also, we took butter and sugar, coffee and canned goods; but when the stores consisted of sacks of beans and flour, or two or three slaughtered steers, we resolutely refrained and went our way, leaving orders to turn such provisions over to the commissary boats whose business was to follow behind us.

My, but the ten of us did live on the fat of the land! For a long time General Kelly vainly tried to head us off. He sent two rowers, in a light, round-bottomed boat, to overtake us and put a stop to our piratical careers. They overtook us all right, but they were two and we were ten. They were empowered by General Kelly to make us prisoners, and they told us so. When we expressed disinclination to become prisoners, they hurried ahead to the next town to invoke the aid of the authorities. We went ashore immediately and cooked an early supper; and under the cloak of darkness we ran by the town and its authorities.

I kept a diary on part of the trip, and as I read it over now I note one persistently recurring phrase, namely, "Living fine." We did live fine. We even disdained to use coffee boiled in water. We made our coffee out of milk, calling the wonderful beverage, if I remember rightly, "pale Vienna."

While we were ahead, skimming the cream, and while the commissary was lost far behind, the main Army, coming along in the middle, starved. This was hard on the Army, I'll allow; but then, the ten of us were individualists. We had initiative and enterprise. We ardently believed that the grub was to the man who got there first, the pale Vienna to the strong. On one stretch the Army went forty-eight hours without grub; and then it arrived at a small village of some three hundred inhabitants, the name of which I do not remember, though I think it was Red Rock. This town, following the practice of all towns through which the Army passed, had appointed a committee of safety. Counting five to a family, Red Rock consisted of sixty households. Her committee of safety was scared stiff by the eruption of two thousand hungry hoboes who lined their boats two and three deep along the river bank. General Kelly was a fair man. He had no intention of working a hardship on the village. He did not expect sixty households to furnish two thousand meals. Besides, the Army had its treasure-chest.

But the committee of safety lost its head. "No encouragement to the invader" was its programme, and when General Kelly wanted to buy food, the committee turned him down. It had nothing to sell; General Kelly's money was "no good" in their burg. And then General Kelly went into action. The bugles blew. The Army left the boats and on top of the bank formed in battle array. The committee was there to see. General Kelly's speech was brief.

"Boys," he said, "when did you eat last?"

"Day before yesterday," they shouted.

"Are you hungry?"

A mighty affirmation from two thousand throats shook the atmosphere. Then General Kelly turned to the committee of safety:—

"You see, gentlemen, the situation. My men have eaten nothing in forty-eight hours. If I turn them loose upon your town, I'll not be responsible for what happens. They are desperate. I offered to buy food for them, but you refused to sell. I now withdraw my offer. Instead, I shall demand. I give you five minutes to decide. Either kill me six steers and give me four thousand rations, or I turn the men loose. Five minutes, gentlemen."

The terrified committee of safety looked at the two thousand hungry hoboes and collapsed. It didn't wait the five minutes. It wasn't going to take any chances. The killing of the steers and the collecting of the requisition began forthwith, and the Army dined.

And still the ten graceless individualists soared along ahead and gathered in everything in sight. But General Kelly fixed us. He sent horsemen down each bank, warning farmers and townspeople against us. They did their work thoroughly, all right. The erstwhile hospitable farmers met us with the icy mit. Also, they summoned the constables when we tied up to the bank, and loosed the dogs. I know. Two of the latter caught me with a barbed-wire fence between me and the river. I was carrying two buckets of milk for the pale Vienna. I didn't damage the fence any; but we drank plebeian coffee boiled with vulgar water, and it was up to me to throw my feet for another pair of trousers. I wonder, gentle reader, if you ever essayed hastily to climb a barbed-wire fence with a bucket of milk in each hand. Ever since that day I have had a prejudice against barbed wire, and I have gathered statistics on the subject.

I was carrying two buckets.

Unable to make an honest living so long as General Kelly kept his two horsemen ahead of us, we returned to the Army and raised a revolution. It was a small affair, but it devastated Company L of the Second Division. The captain of Company L refused to recognize us; said we were deserters, and traitors, and scalawags; and when he drew rations for Company L from the commissary, he wouldn't give us any. That captain didn't appreciate us, or he wouldn't have refused us grub. Promptly we intrigued with the first lieutenant. He joined us with the ten men in his boat, and in return we elected him captain of Company M. The captain of Company L raised a roar. Down upon us came General Kelly, Colonel Speed, and Colonel Baker. The twenty of us stood firm, and our revolution was ratified.

But we never bothered with the commissary. Our hustlers drew better rations from the farmers. Our new captain, however, doubted us. He never knew when he'd see the ten of us again, once we got under way in the morning, so he called in a blacksmith to clinch his captaincy. In the stern of our boat, one on each side, were driven two heavy eye-bolts of iron. Correspondingly, on the bow of his boat, were fastened two huge iron hooks. The boats were brought together, end on, the hooks dropped into the eye-bolts, and there we were, hard and fast. We couldn't lose that captain. But we were irrepressible. Out of our very manacles we wrought an invincible device that enabled us to put it all over every other boat in the fleet.

Like all great inventions, this one of ours was accidental. We discovered it the first time we ran on a snag in a bit of a rapid. The head-boat hung up and anchored, and the tail-boat swung around in the current, pivoting the head-boat on the snag. I was at the stern of the tail-boat, steering. In vain we tried to shove off. Then I ordered the men from the head-boat into the tail-boat. Immediately the head-boat floated clear, and its men returned into it. After that, snags, reefs, shoals, and bars had no terrors for us. The instant the head-boat struck, the men in it leaped into the tail-boat. Of course, the head-boat floated over the obstruction and the tail-boat then struck. Like automatons, the twenty men now in the tail-boat leaped into the head-boat, and the tail-boat floated past.

The boats used by the Army were all alike, made by the mile and sawed off. They were flat-boats, and their lines were rectangles. Each boat was six feet wide, ten feet long, and a foot and a half deep. Thus, when our two boats were hooked together, I sat at the stern steering a craft twenty feet long, containing twenty husky hoboes who "spelled" each other at the oars and paddles, and loaded with blankets, cooking outfit, and our own private commissary.

Still we caused General Kelly trouble. He had called in his horsemen, and substituted three police-boats that travelled in the van and allowed no boats to pass them. The craft containing Company M crowded the police-boats hard. We could have passed them easily, but it was against the rules. So we kept a respectful distance astern and waited. Ahead we knew was virgin farming country, unbegged and generous; but we waited. White water was all we needed, and when we rounded a bend and a rapid showed up we knew what would happen. Smash! Police-boat number one goes on a boulder and hangs up. Bang! Police-boat number two follows suit. Whop! Police-boat number three encounters the common fate of all. Of course our boat does the same things; but one, two, the men are out of the head-boat and into the tail-boat; one, two, they are out of the tail-boat and into the head-boat; and one, two, the men who belong in the tail-boat are back in it and we are dashing on. "Stop! you blankety-blank-blanks!" shriek the police-boats. "How can we?—blank the blankety-blank river, anyway!" we wail plaintively as we surge past, caught in that remorseless current that sweeps us on out of sight and into the hospitable farmer-country that replenishes our private commissary with the cream of its contributions. Again we drink pale Vienna and realize that the grub is to the man who gets there.

Poor General Kelly! He devised another scheme. The whole fleet started ahead of us. Company M of the Second Division started in its proper place in the line, which was last. And it took us only one day to put the "kibosh" on that particular scheme. Twenty-five miles of bad water lay before us—all rapids, shoals, bars, and boulders. It was over that stretch of water that the oldest inhabitants of Des Moines had shaken their heads. Nearly two hundred boats entered the bad water ahead of us, and they piled up in the most astounding manner. We went through that stranded fleet like hemlock through the fire. There was no avoiding the boulders, bars, and snags except by getting out on the bank. We didn't avoid them. We went right over them, one, two, one, two, head-boat, tail-boat, head-boat, tail-boat, all hands back and forth and back again. We camped that night alone, and loafed in camp all of next day while the Army patched and repaired its wrecked boats and straggled up to us.

There was no stopping our cussedness. We rigged up a mast, piled on the canvas (blankets), and travelled short hours while the Army worked over-time to keep us in sight. Then General Kelly had recourse to diplomacy. No boat could touch us in the straight-away. Without discussion, we were the hottest bunch that ever came down the Des Moines, The ban of the police-boats was lifted. Colonel Speed was put aboard, and with this distinguished officer we had the honor of arriving first at Keokuk on the Mississippi. And right here I want to say to General Kelly and Colonel Speed that here's my hand. You were heroes, both of you, and you were men. And I'm sorry for at least ten per cent of the trouble that was given you by the head-boat of Company M.

At Keokuk the whole fleet was lashed together in a huge raft, and, after being wind-bound a day, a steamboat took us in tow down the Mississippi to Quincy, Illinois, where we camped across the river on Goose Island. Here the raft idea was abandoned, the boats being joined together in groups of four and decked over. Somebody told me that Quincy was the richest town of its size in the United States. When I heard this, I was immediately overcome by an irresistible impulse to throw my feet. No "blowed-in-the-glass profesh" could possibly pass up such a promising burg. I crossed the river to Quincy in a small dug-out; but I came back in a large riverboat, down to the gunwales with the results of my thrown feet.[1] Of course I kept all the money I had collected, though I paid the boat-hire; also I took my pick of the underwear, socks, cast-off clothes, shirts, "kicks," and "sky-pieces"; and when Company M had taken all it wanted there was still a respectable heap that was turned over to Company L. Alas, I was young and prodigal in those days! I told a thousand "stories" to the good people of Quincy, and every story was "good"; but since I have come to write for the magazines I have often regretted the wealth of story, the fecundity of fiction, I lavished that day in Quincy, Illinois.

It was at Hannibal, Missouri, that the ten invincibles went to pieces. It was not planned. We just naturally flew apart. The Boiler-Maker and I deserted secretly. On the same day Scotty and Davy

I took my pick.

made a swift sneak for the Illinois shore; also McAvoy and Fish achieved their get-away. This accounts for six of the ten; what became of the remaining four I do not know. As a sample of life on The Road, I make the following quotation from my diary of the several days following my desertion.

"Friday, May 25th. Boiler-Maker and I left the camp on the island. We went ashore on the Illinois side in a skiff and walked six miles on the C.B. & Q. to Fell Creek.[2] We had gone six miles out of our way, but we got on a hand-car and rode six miles to Hull's, on the Wabash. While there, we met McAvoy, Fish, Scotty, and Davy, who had also pulled out from the Army.

"Saturday, May 26th. At 2.11 A.M. we caught the Cannon-ball as she slowed up at the crossing.[3] Scotty and Davy were ditched. The four of us were ditched at the Bluffs, forty miles farther on. In the afternoon Fish and McAvoy caught a freight while Boiler-Maker and I were away getting something to eat.

"Sunday, May 27th. At 3.21 A.M. we caught the Cannon-ball and found Scotty and Davy on the blind. We were all ditched at daylight at Jacksonville. The C. & A. runs through here, and we're going to take that.[4] Boiler-Maker went off, but didn't return. Guess he caught a freight.

"Monday, May 28th. Boiler-Maker didn't show up. Scotty and Davy went off to sleep somewhere, and didn't get back in time to catch the K.C. passenger at 3.30 A.M. I caught her and rode her till after sunrise to Masson City, 25,000 inhabitants.[5] Caught a cattle train and rode all night.

"Tuesday, May 29th. Arrived in Chicago at 7 A.M. . . ."

And years afterward, in China, I had the grief of learning that the device we employed to navigate the rapids of the Des Moines—the one-two-one-two, head-boat-tail-boat proposition—was not originated by us. I learned that the Chinese river-boatmen had for thousands of years used a similar device to negotiate "bad water." It is a good stunt all right, even if we don't get the credit. It answers Dr. Jordan's test of truth: "Will it work? Will you trust your life to it?"[6]

BULLS

If the tramp were suddenly to pass away from the United States, widespread misery for many families would follow. The tramp enables thousands of men to earn honest livings, educate their children, and bring them up God-fearing and industrious. I know. At one time my father was a constable and hunted tramps for a living. The community paid him so much per head for all the tramps he could catch, and also, I believe, he got mileage fees. Ways and means was always a pressing problem in our household, and the amount of meat on the table, the new pair of shoes, the day's outing, or the textbook for school, were dependent upon my father's luck in the chase. Well I remember the suppressed eagerness and the suspense with which I waited to learn each morning what the results of his past night's toil had been—how many tramps he had gathered in and what the chances were for convicting them. And so it was, when later, as a tramp, I succeeded in eluding some predatory constable, I could not but feel sorry for the little boys and girls at home in that constable's house; it seemed to me in a way that I was defrauding those little boys and girls of some of the good things of life.

But it's all in the game. The hobo defies society, and society's watch-dogs make a living out of him. Some hoboes like to be caught by the watch-dogs—especially in winter-time. Of course, such hoboes select communities where the jails are "good," wherein no work is performed and the food is substantial. Also, there have been, and most probably still are, constables who divide their fees with the hoboes they arrest. Such a constable does not have to hunt. He whistles, and the game comes right up to his hand. It is surprising, the money that is made out of stone-broke tramps. All through the South—at least when I was hoboing—are convict camps and plantations, where the time of convicted hoboes is bought by the farmers, and where the hoboes simply have to work. Then there are places like the quarries at Rutland, Vermont, where the hobo is exploited, the unearned energy in his body, which he has accumulated by "battering on the drag" or "slamming gates," being extracted for the benefit of that particular community.

Now I don't know anything about the quarries at Rutland, Vermont. I'm very glad that I don't, when I remember how near I was to getting into them. Tramps pass the word along, and I first heard of those quarries when I was in Indiana. But when I got into New England, I heard of them continually, and always with danger-signals flying. "They want men in the quarries," the passing hoboes said; "and they never give a 'stiff' less than ninety days." By the time I got into New Hampshire I was pretty well keyed up over those quarries, and I fought shy of railroad cops, "bulls," and constables as I never had before.

One evening I went down to the railroad yards at Concord and found a freight train made up and ready to start. I located an empty box-car, slid open the side-door, and climbed in. It was my hope to win across to White River by morning; that would bring me into Vermont and not more than a thousand miles from Rutland. But after that, as I worked north, the distance between me and the point of danger would begin to increase. In the car I found a "gay-cat," who displayed unusual trepidation at my entrance. He took me for a "shack" (brakeman), and when he learned I was only a stiff, he began talking about the quarries at Rutland as the cause of the fright I had given him. He was a young country fellow, and had beaten his way only over local stretches of road.

The freight got under way, and we lay down in one end of the box-car and went to sleep. Two or three hours afterward, at a stop, I was awakened by the noise of the right-hand door being softly slid open. The gay-cat slept on. I made no movement, though I veiled my eyes with my lashes to a little slit through which I could see out.

A lantern was thrust in through the doorway, followed by the head of a shack. He discovered us, and looked at us for a moment. I was prepared for a violent expression on his part, or the customary "Hit the grit, you son of a toad!" Instead of this he cautiously withdrew the lantern and very, very softly slid the door to. This struck me as eminently unusual and suspicious. I listened, and softly I heard the hasp drop into place. The door was latched on the outside. We could not open it from the inside. One way of sudden exit from that car was blocked. It would never do. I waited a few seconds, then crept to the left-hand door and tried it. It was not yet latched. I opened it, dropped to the ground, and closed it behind me. Then I passed across the bumpers to the other side of the train. I opened the door the shack had latched, climbed in, and closed it behind me. Both exits were available again. The gay-cat was still asleep.

The train got under way. It came to the next stop. I heard footsteps in the gravel. Then the left-hand door was thrown open noisily. The gay-cat awoke, I made believe to awake; and we sat up and stared at the shack and his lantern. He didn't waste any time getting down to business.

"I want three dollars," he said.

We got on our feet and came nearer to him to confer. We expressed an absolute and devoted willingness to give him three dollars, but explained our wretched luck that compelled our desire to remain unsatisfied. The shack was incredulous. He dickered with us. He would compromise for two dollars. We regretted our condition of poverty. He said uncomplimentary things, called us sons of toads, and damned us from hell to breakfast. Then he threatened. He explained that if we didn't dig up, he'd lock us in and carry us on to White River and turn us over to the authorities. He also explained all about the quarries at Rutland.

Now that shack thought he had us dead to rights. Was not he guarding the one door, and had he not himself latched the opposite door but a few minutes before? When he began talking about quarries, the frightened gay-cat started to sidle across to the other door. The shack laughed loud and long. "Don't be in a hurry," he said; "I locked that door on the outside at the last stop." So implicitly did he believe the door to be locked that his words carried conviction. The gay-cat believed and was in despair.

The shack delivered his ultimatum. Either we should dig up two dollars, or he would lock us in and turn us over to the constable at White River—and that meant ninety days and the quarries. Now, gentle reader, just suppose that the other door had been locked. Behold the precariousness of human life. For lack of a dollar, I'd have gone to the quarries and served three months as a convict slave. So would the gay-cat. Count me out, for I was hopeless; but consider the gay-cat. He might have come out, after those ninety days, pledged to a life of crime. And later he might have broken your skull, even your skull, with a blackjack in an endeavor to take possession of the money on your person—and if not your skull, then some other poor and unoffending creature's skull.

But the door was unlocked, and I alone knew it. The gay-cat and I begged for mercy. I joined in the pleading and wailing out of sheer cussedness, I suppose. But I did my best. I told a "story" that would have melted the heart of any mug; but it didn't melt the heart of that sordid money-grasper of a shack. When he became convinced that we didn't have any money, he slid the door shut and latched it, then lingered a moment on the chance that we had fooled him and that we would now offer him the two dollars.

Then it was that I let out a few links. I called *him* a son of a toad. I called him all the other things he had called me. And then I called him a few additional things. I came from the West, where men knew how to swear, and I wasn't going to let any mangy shack on a measly New England "jerk" put it over me in vividness and vigor of language. At first the shack tried to laugh it down. Then he made the mistake of attempting to reply. I let out a few more links, and I cut him to the raw and therein rubbed winged and flaming epithets. Nor was my fine frenzy all whim and literary; I was indignant at this vile creature, who, in default of a dollar, would consign me to three months of slavery. Furthermore, I had a sneaking idea that he got a "drag" out of the constable fees.

But I fixed him. I lacerated his feelings and pride several dollars' worth. He tried to scare me by threatening to come in after me and kick the stuffing out of me. In return, I promised to kick him in the face while he was climbing in. The advantage of position was with me, and he saw it. So he kept the door shut and called for help from the rest of the train-crew. I could hear them answering and crunching through the gravel to him. And all the time the other door was unlatched, and they didn't know it; and in the meantime the gay-cat was ready to die with fear.

"Oh, I was a hero—with my line of retreat straight behind me. I slanged the shack and his mates till they threw the door open and I could see their infuriated faces in the shine of the lanterns. It was all very simple to them. They had us cornered in the car, and they were going to come in and manhandle us. They started. I didn't kick anybody in the face. I jerked the opposite door open, and the gay-cat and I went out. The train-crew took after us.

We went over—if I remember correctly—a stone fence. But I have no doubts of recollection about where we found ourselves. In the darkness I promptly fell over a grave-stone. The gay-cat sprawled over another. And then we got the chase of our lives through that graveyard. The ghosts must have thought we were going some. So did the train-crew, for when we emerged from the graveyard and plunged across a road into a dark wood, the shacks gave up the pursuit and went back to their train. A little later that night the gay-cat and I found ourselves at the well of a farmhouse. We were after a drink of water, but we noticed a small rope that ran down one side of the well. We hauled it up and found on the end of it a gallon-can of cream. And that is as near as I got to the quarries of Rutland, Vermont.

When hoboes pass the word along, concerning a town, that "the bulls is horstile," avoid that town, or, if you must, go through softly. There are some towns that one must always go through softly. Such a town was Cheyenne, on the Union Pacific. It had a national reputation for being "horstile,"—and it was all due to the efforts of one Jeff Carr (if I remember his name aright). Jeff Carr could size up the "front" of a hobo on the instant. He never entered into discussion. In the one moment he sized up the hobo, and in the next he struck out with both fists, a club, or anything else he had handy. After he had manhandled the hobo, he started him out of town with a promise of worse if he ever saw him again. Jeff Carr knew the game. North, south, east, and west to the uttermost confines of the United States (Canada and Mexico included), the man-handled hoboes carried the word that Cheyenne was "horstile." Fortunately, I never encountered Jeff Carr. I passed though Cheyenne in a blizzard. There were eighty-four hoboes with me at the time. The strength of numbers made us pretty nonchalant on most things, but not on Jeff Carr. The connotation of "Jeff Carr" stunned our imagination, numbed our virility, and the whole gang was mortally scared of meeting him.

It rarely pays to stop and enter into explanations with bulls when they look "horstile." A swift get-away is the thing to do. It took me some time to learn this; but the finishing touch was put upon me by a bull in New York City. Ever since that time it has been an automatic process with me to make a run for it when I see a bull reaching for me. This automatic process has become a mainspring of conduct in me, wound up and ready for instant release. I shall never get over it. Should I be eighty years old, hobbling along the street on crutches, and should a policeman suddenly reach out for me, I know I'd drop the crutches and run like a deer.

The finishing touch to my education in bulls was received on a hot summer afternoon in New York City. It was during a week of scorching weather. I had got into the habit of throwing my feet in the morning, and of spending the afternoon in the little park that is hard by Newspaper Row and the City Hall. It was near there that I could buy from push-cart men current books (that had been injured in the making or binding) for a few cents each. Then, right in the park itself, were little booths where one could buy glorious, ice-cold, sterilized milk and buttermilk at a penny a glass. Every afternoon I sat on a bench and read, and went on a milk debauch. I got away with from five to ten glasses each afternoon. It was dreadfully hot weather.

So here I was, a meek and studious milk-drinking hobo, and behold what I got for it. One afternoon I arrived at the park, a fresh book-purchase under my arm and a tremendous buttermilk thirst under my shirt. In the middle of the street, in front of the City Hall, I noticed, as I came along heading for the buttermilk booth, that a crowd had formed. It was right where I was crossing the street, so I stopped to see the cause of the collection of curious men. At first I could see nothing. Then, from the sounds I heard and from a glimpse I caught, I knew that it was a bunch of gamins playing pee-wee.[1] Now pee-wee is not permitted in the streets of New York. I didn't know that, but I learned pretty lively. I had paused possibly thirty seconds, in which time I had learned the cause of the crowd, when I heard a gamin yell "Bull!" The gamins knew their business. They ran. I didn't.

The crowd broke up immediately and started for the sidewalk on both sides of the street. I started for the sidewalk on the park-side. There must have been fifty men, who had been in the original

One afternoon I arrived at the park.

crowd, who were heading in the same direction. We were loosely strung out. I noticed the bull, a strapping policeman in a gray suit. He was coming along the middle of the street, without haste, merely sauntering. I noticed casually that he changed his course, and was heading obliquely for the same sidewalk that I was heading for directly. He sauntered along, threading the strung-out crowd, and I noticed that his course and mine would cross each other. I was so innocent of wrong-doing that, in spite of my education in bulls and their ways, I apprehended nothing. I never dreamed that bull was after me. Out of my respect for the law I was actually all ready to pause the next moment and let him cross in front of me. The pause came all right, but it was not of my volition; also it was a backward pause. Without warning, that bull had suddenly launched out at me on the chest with both hands. At the same moment, verbally, he cast the bar sinister on my genealogy.

All my free American blood boiled. All my liberty-loving ancestors clamored in me. "What do you mean?" I demanded. You see, I wanted an explanation. And I got it. Bang! His club came down on top of my head, and I was reeling backward like a drunken man, the curious faces of the onlookers billowing up and down like the waves of the sea, my precious book falling from under my arm into the dirt, the bull advancing with the club ready for another blow. And in that dizzy moment I had a vision. I saw that club descending many times upon my head; I saw myself, bloody and battered and hard-looking, in a police-court; I heard a charge of disorderly conduct, profane language, resisting an officer, and a few other things, read by a clerk; and I saw myself across in Blackwell's Island. Oh, I knew the game. If lost all interest in explanations. I didn't stop to pick up my precious, unread book. I turned and ran. I was pretty sick, but I ran. And run I shall, to my dying day, whenever a bull begins to explain with a club.

Why, years after my tramping days, when I was a student in the University of California, one night I went to the circus. After the show and the concert I lingered on to watch the working of the transportation machinery of a great circus. The circus was leaving that night. By a bonfire I came upon a bunch of small boys. There

I saw myself across in Blackwell's Island.

were about twenty of them, and as they talked with one another I learned that they were going to run away with the circus. Now the circus-men didn't want to be bothered with this mess of urchins, and a telephone to police headquarters had "coppered" the play. A squad of ten policemen had been despatched to the scene to arrest the small boys for violating the nine o'clock curfew ordinance. The policemen

By a bonfire.

surrounded the bonfire, and crept up close to it in the darkness. At the signal, they made a rush, each policeman grabbing at the youngsters as he would grab into a basket of squirming eels.

Now I didn't know anything about the coming of the police; and when I saw the sudden eruption of brass-buttoned, helmeted bulls, each of them reaching with both hands, all the forces and stability of my being were overthrown. Remained only the automatic process to run. And I ran. I didn't know I was running. I didn't know anything. It was, as I have said, automatic. There was no reason for me to run. I was not a hobo. I was a citizen of that community. It was my home town. I was guilty of no wrong-doing. I was a college man. I had even got my name in the papers, and I wore good clothes that had never been slept in. And yet I ran—blindly, madly, like a startled deer, for over a block. And when I came to myself, I noted that I was still running. It required a positive effort of will to stop those legs of mine.

No, I'll never get over it. I can't help it. When a bull reaches, I run. Besides, I have an unhappy faculty for getting into jail. I have been in jail more times since I was a hobo than when I was one. I start out on a Sunday morning with a young lady on a bicycle ride. Before we can get outside the city limits we are arrested for passing a pedestrian on the sidewalk. I resolve to be more careful. The next time I am on a bicycle it is night-time and my acetylene-gas-lamp is misbehaving. I cherish the sickly flame carefully, because of the ordinance. I am in a hurry, but I ride at a snail's pace so as not to jar out the flickering flame. I reach the city limits; I am beyond the jurisdiction of the ordinance; and I proceed to scorch to make up for lost time. And half a mile farther on I am "pinched" by a bull, and the next morning I forfeit my bail in the police court. The city had treacherously extended its limits into a mile of the country, and I didn't know, that was all. I remember my inalienable right of free speech and peaceable assemblage, and I get up on a soap-box to trot out the particular economic bees that buzz in my bonnet, and a bull takes me off that box and leads me to the city prison, and after that I get out on bail. It's no use. In Korea I used to be arrested about every other day. It was the same thing in Manchuria. The last time I was in Japan I broke into jail under the pretext of being a Russian spy. It wasn't my pretext, but it got me into jail just the same. There is no hope for me. I am fated to do the Prisoner-of-Chillon stunt yet.[2] This is prophecy.

I once hypnotized a bull on Boston Common. It was past midnight and he had me dead to rights; but before I got done with him he had ponied up a silver quarter and given me the address of an all-night restaurant. Then there was a bull in Bristol, New Jersey, who caught me and let me go, and heaven knows he had provocation enough to put me in jail. I hit him the hardest I'll wager he was ever hit in his life. It happened this way. About midnight I nailed a freight out of Philadelphia. The shacks ditched me. She was pulling out slowly through the maze of tracks and switches of the freight-yards. I nailed her again, and again I was ditched. You see, I had to nail her "outside," for she was a through freight with every door locked and sealed.

The second time I was ditched the shack gave me a lecture. He told me I was risking my life, that it was a fast freight and that she went some. I told him I was used to going some myself, but it was no go. He said he wouldn't permit me to commit suicide, and I hit the grit. But I nailed her a third time, getting in between on the bumpers. They were the most meagre bumpers I had ever seen—I do not refer to the real bumpers, the iron bumpers that are connected by the coupling-link and that pound and grind on each other; what I refer to are the beams, like huge cleats, that cross the ends of freight cars just above the bumpers. When one rides the bumpers, he stands on these cleats, one foot on each, the bumpers between his feet and just beneath.

But the beams or cleats I found myself on were not the broad, generous ones that at that time were usually on box-cars. On the contrary, they were very narrow—not more than an inch and a half in breadth. I couldn't get half of the width of my sole on them. Then there was nothing to which to hold with my hands. True, there were the ends of the two box-cars; but those ends were flat, perpendicular surfaces. There were no grips. I could only press the flats of my palms against the car-ends for support. But that would have been all right if the cleats for my feet had been decently wide.

As the freight got out of Philadelphia she began to hit up speed. Then I understood what the shack had meant by suicide. The freight went faster and faster. She was a through freight, and there was nothing to stop her. On that section of the Pennsylvania four tracks run side by side, and my east-bound freight didn't need to worry about passing west-bound freights, nor about being overtaken by east-bound expresses. She had the track to herself, and she used it. I was in a precarious situation. I stood with the mere edges of my feet on the narrow projections, the palms of my hands pressing desperately against the flat, perpendicular ends of each car. And those cars moved, and moved individually, up and down and back and forth. Did you ever see a circus rider, standing on two running horses, with one foot on the back of each horse? Well, that was what I was doing, with several differences. The circus rider had the reins to hold on to, while I had nothing; he stood on the broad soles of his feet, while I stood on the edges of mine; he bent his legs and body, gaining the strength of the arch in his posture and achieving the stability of a low centre of gravity, while I was compelled to stand upright and keep my legs straight; he rode face forward, while I was riding sidewise; and also, if he fell off, he'd get only a roll in the sawdust, while I'd have been ground to pieces beneath the wheels.

And that freight was certainly going some, roaring and shrieking, swinging madly around curves, thundering over trestles, one car-end bumping up when the other was jarring down, or jerking to the right at the same moment the other was lurching to the left, and with me all the while praying and hoping for the train to stop. But she didn't stop. She didn't have to. For the first, last, and only time on The Road, I got all I wanted. I abandoned the bumpers and managed to get out on a side-ladder; it was ticklish work, for I had never encountered car-ends that were so parsimonious of hand-holds and foot-holds as those car-ends were.

I heard the engine whistling, and I felt the speed easing down. I knew the train wasn't going to stop, but my mind was made up to chance it if she slowed down sufficiently. The right of way at this point took a curve, crossed a bridge over a canal, and cut through the town of Bristol. This combination compelled slow speed. I clung on to the side-ladder and waited. I didn't know it was the town of Bristol we were approaching. I did not know what necessitated slackening in speed. All I knew was that I wanted to get off. I strained my eyes in the darkness for a street-crossing on which to land. I was pretty well down the train, and before my car was in the town the engine was past the station and I could feel her making speed again.

Then came the street. It was too dark to see how wide it was or what was on the other side. I knew I needed all of that street if I was to remain on my feet after I struck. I dropped off on the near side. It sounds easy. By "dropped off" I mean just this: I first of all, on the side-ladder, thrust my body forward as far as I could in the direction the train was going—this to give as much space as possible in which to gain backward momentum when I swung off. Then I swung, swung out and backward, backward with all my might, and let go— at the same time throwing myself backward as if I intended to strike the ground on the back of my head. The whole effort was to overcome as much as possible the primary forward momentum the train had imparted to my body. When my feet hit the grit, my body was lying backward on the air at an angle of forty-five degrees. I had reduced the forward momentum some, for when my feet struck, I did not immediately pitch forward on my face. Instead, my body rose to the perpendicular and began to incline forward. In point of fact, my body proper still retained much momentum, while my feet, through contact with the earth, had lost all their momentum. This momentum the feet had lost I had to supply anew by lifting them as rapidly as I could and running them forward in order to keep them under my forward-moving body. The result was that my feet beat a rapid and explosive tattoo clear across the street. I didn't dare stop them. If I had, I'd have pitched forward. It was up to me to keep on going.

I was an involuntary projectile, worrying about what was on the other side of the street and hoping that it wouldn't be a stone wall or a telegraph pole. And just then I hit something. Horrors! I saw it just the instant before the disaster—of all things, a bull, standing there in the darkness. We went down together, rolling over and over; and the automatic process was such in that miserable creature that in the moment of impact he reached out and clutched me and never let go. We were both knocked out, and he held on to a very lamb-like hobo while he recovered.

If that bull had any imagination, he must have thought me a traveller from other worlds, the man from Mars just arriving; for in the darkness he hadn't seen me swing from the train. In fact, his first words were: "Where did you come from?" His next words, and before I had time to answer, were: "I've a good mind to run you in." This latter, I am convinced, was likewise automatic. He was a really good bull at heart, for after I had told him a "story" and helped brush off his clothes, he gave me until the next freight to get out of town. I stipulated two things: first, that the freight be east-bound, and second, that it should not be a through freight with all doors sealed and locked. To this he agreed, and thus, by the terms of the Treaty of Bristol, I escaped being pinched.

I remember another night, in that part of the country, when I just missed another bull. If I had hit him, I'd have telescoped him, for I was coming down from above, all holds free, with several other bulls one jump behind and reaching for me. This is how it happened. I had been lodging in a livery stable in Washington. I had a box-stall and unnumbered horse-blankets all to myself. In return for such sumptuous accommodation I took care of a string of horses each morning. I might have been there yet, if it hadn't been for the bulls.

One evening, about nine o'clock, I returned to the stable to go to bed, and found a crap game in full blast. It had been a market day, and all the negroes had money. It would be well to explain the lay of the land. The livery stable faced on two streets. I entered the front, passed through the office, and came to the alley between two rows of stalls that ran the length of the building and opened out on the other street. Midway along this alley, beneath a gas-jet and between the rows of horses, were about forty negroes. I joined them as an onlooker. I was broke and couldn't play. A coon was making passes and not dragging down.[3] He was riding his luck, and with each pass the total stake doubled. All kinds of money lay on the floor. It was fascinating. With each pass, the chances increased tremendously against the coon making another pass. The excitement was intense.

And just then there came a thundering smash on the big doors that opened on the back street.

A few of the negroes bolted in the opposite direction. I paused from my flight a moment to grab at the all kinds of money on the floor. This wasn't theft: it was merely custom. Every man who hadn't run was grabbing. The doors crashed open and swung in, and through them surged a squad of bulls. We surged the other way. It was dark in the office, and the narrow door would not permit all of us to pass out to the street at the same time. Things became congested. A coon took a dive through the window, taking the sash along with him and followed by other coons. At our rear, the bulls were nailing prisoners. A big coon and myself made a dash at the door at the same time. He was bigger than I, and he pivoted me and got through first. The next instant a club swatted him on the head and he went down like a steer. Another squad of bulls was waiting outside for us. They knew they couldn't stop the rush with their hands, and so they were swinging their clubs. I stumbled over the fallen coon who had pivoted me, ducked a swat from a club, dived between a bull's legs, and was free. And then how I ran! There was a lean mulatto just in front of me, and I took his pace. He knew the town better than I did, and I knew that in the way he ran lay safety. But he, on the other hand, took me for a pursuing bull. He never looked around. He just ran. My wind was good, and I hung on to his pace and nearly killed him. In the end he stumbled weakly, went down on his knees, and surrendered to me. And when he discovered I wasn't a bull, all that saved me was that he didn't have any wind left in him.

That was why I left Washington—not on account of the mulatto, but on account of the bulls. I went down to the depot and caught the first blind out on a Pennsylvania Railroad express. After the train got good and under way and I noted the speed she was making, a misgiving smote me. This was a four-track railroad, and the engines took water on the fly. Hoboes had long since warned me never to ride the first blind on trains where the engines took water on the fly. And now let me explain. Between the tracks are shallow metal troughs. As the engine, at full speed, passes above, a sort of chute drops down into the trough. The result is that all the water in the trough rushes up the chute and fills the tender.

I went down to the depot and caught the first blind out.

Somewhere along between Washington and Baltimore, as I sat on the platform of the blind, a fine spray began to fill the air. It did no harm. Ah, ha, thought I; it's all a bluff, this taking water on the fly being bad for the bo on the first blind. What does this little spray amount to? Then I began to marvel at the device. This *was* railroading! Talk about your primitive Western railroading—and just then the tender filled up, and it hadn't reached the end of the trough. A tidal wave of water poured over the back of the tender and down upon me. I was soaked to the skin, as wet as if I had fallen overboard.

The train pulled into Baltimore. As is the custom in the great Eastern cities, the railroad ran beneath the level of the streets on the bottom of a big "cut." As the train pulled into the lighted depot, I made myself as small as possible on the blind. But a railroad bull saw me, and gave chase. Two more joined him. I was past the depot, and I ran straight on down the track. I was in a sort of trap. On each side of me rose the steep walls of the cut, and if I ever essayed them and failed, I knew that I'd slide back into the clutches of the bulls. I ran on and on, studying the walls of the cut for a favorable place to climb up. At last I saw such a place. It came just after I had passed under a bridge that carried a level street across the cut. Up the steep slope I went, clawing hand and foot. The three railroad bulls were clawing up right after me.

At the top, I found myself in a vacant lot. On one side was a low wall that separated it from the street. There was no time for minute investigation. They were at my heels. I headed for the wall and vaulted it. And right there was where I got the surprise of my life. One is used to thinking that one side of a wall is just as high as the other side. But that wall was different. You see, the vacant lot was much higher than the level of the street. On my side the wall was low, but on the other side—well, as I came soaring over the top, all holds free, it seemed to me that I was falling feet-first, plump into an abyss. There beneath me, on the sidewalk, under the light of a street-lamp was a bull. I guess it was nine or ten feet down to the sidewalk; but in the shock of surprise in mid-air it seemed twice that distance.

I straightened out in the air and came down. At first I thought I was going to land on the bull. My clothes did brush him as my feet struck the sidewalk with explosive impact. It was a wonder he didn't drop dead, for he hadn't heard me coming. It was the man-from-Mars stunt over again. The bull did jump. He shied away from me like a horse from an auto; and then he reached for me. I didn't stop to explain. I left that to my pursuers, who were dropping over the wall rather gingerly. But I got a chase all right. I ran up one street and down another, dodged around corners, and at last got away.

After spending some of the coin I'd got from the crap game and killing off an hour of time, I came back to the railroad cut, just outside the lights of the depot, and waited for a train. My blood had cooled down, and I shivered miserably, what of my wet clothes. At last a train pulled into the station. I lay low in the darkness, and successfully boarded her when she pulled out, taking good care this time to make the second blind. No more water on the fly in mine. The train ran forty miles to the first stop. I got off in a lighted depot that was strangely familiar. I was back in Washington. In some way, during the excitement of the get-away in Baltimore, running through strange streets, dodging and turning and retracing, I had got turned around. I had taken the train out the wrong way. I had lost a night's sleep, I had been soaked to the skin, I had been chased for my life; and for all my pains I was back where I had started. Oh, no, life on The Road is not all beer and skittles. But I didn't go back to the livery stable. I had done some pretty successful grabbing, and I didn't want to reckon up with the coons. So I caught the next train out, and ate my breakfast in Baltimore.

Explanatory Notes

EPIGRAPH

1. *Sestina of the Tramp-Royal*: Poem by Rudyard Kipling (1865–1936), published in 1896.

DEDICATION

1. Josiah Flynt was the pen name of Josiah Flynt Willard (1869–1907), an undercover investigator of tramp life who was secretly addicted to tramping. His book *Tramping with the Tramps: Studies and Sketches of Vagabond Life* (1899) was the authoritative book on the subject for a generation.

CONFESSION

1. John Law: Hobo slang for police or law enforcement.

2. blind baggage: Platform at the end of a mail or baggage car (usually behind the engine); platform is "blind" because there is no door leading out to it.

3. Cerberus: A vicious three-headed dog who guards Hades in Greek mythology.

4. "Rangoon, and China, and . . . around the Horn": Rangoon is the former capital of Burma, now known as Yangon, capital of Myanmar. The "Horn" is Cape Horn at the southernmost tip of South America, around which ships passed between the Pacific and the Atlantic.

5. Mrs. Grundy: A fabled busybody in English popular culture who prudishly guards conventional morality; created by playwright Thomas Morton (1764–1838) in *Speed the Plough* (1798).

HOLDING HER DOWN

1. jerk: A seldom-used local branch of a railroad line. Refers to "jerking a drink," which means putting water into the steam locomotive; a "jerkwater" was where trains stopped only for watering.

2. two-bits: slang for twenty-five cents.

3. "ten little niggers": Title of a popular nineteenth-century English nursery rhyme about black children who die one by one. The rhyme reflects the racist violence that informed nineteenth-century British imperialism. In the United States, the rhyme was commonly adapted to "Ten Little Indians."

4. gay-cats: Slang term for newcomers to the road.

5. Croesus: King of Lydia, in Asia Minor, in the sixth century B.C.E.; renowned for his wealth.

6. Pullmans: The luxurious passenger cars built by the Pullman Palace Car Company; founded by George M. Pullman (1831–1897) in 1867.

PICTURES

1. coon: Racial epithet for African Americans derived from the word "raccoon"; prior to the mid-nineteenth century, "coon" was a word that denoted a clever person or trickster.

2. "Not the wealth of Ormuz and of Ind, nor the pressure of a pneumatic ram": "Ormuz" was the prosperous island port in the Strait of Hormoz off the coast of present-day Iran, between the Persian Gulf and the Gulf of Oman; also known as Hormoz and Hormuz. "Ind" refers to ancient India, legendary for its wealth. A "pneumatic ram" is a compressed-air machine used to break rock, especially in mining.

"PINCHED"

1. fly-cop: A police detective.

2. driven team: Driven a team of horses.

3. habeas corpus: Latin phrase translated literally as "you have the body." The phrase appears in the Constitution of the United States guaranteeing the right of a person detained or arrested to appear in court to ensure that the custody is lawful.

4. Fra Lippo Lippi: Title of poem by Robert Browning (1812–1889), published in 1855, about a fifteenth-century Italian monk who was taken into a convent as an orphan and made to renounce the world in exchange for steady meals. He later became an artist whose realism conflicted with the Catholic Church's religious ideals.

5. "Kipling's heroes who stormed Lungtungpen": In Rudyard Kipling's humorous short story "The Taking of Lungtungpen" (1888), an Irish soldier tells how he and his men captured a Burmese town naked in order to surprise its defenders.

6. Prometheus: God of Greek mythology who stole fire from the gods and gave it to humans; Zeus punished Prometheus by chaining him to a rock and sending an eagle to eat his liver.

7. pannikins: Small tin pans or cups.

8. "Like Childe Roland, dauntless the slug-horn to his lips he bore": London paraphrases the final lines of Robert Browning's bleak epic poem, "Childe Roland to the Dark Tower Came" (1855). In the poem, Childe Roland, a knight in training, approaches the ominous Dark Tower and blows his horn, a traditional call to battle.

9. stay-bolts: Rods used in steam boilers to prevent the sides from blowing or bulging.

10. Lexow Committee: Committee formed in 1894 by New York state senator Clarence Lexow to investigate corruption and brutality in the New York City police department; the committee issued its scathing report in 1895.

THE PEN

1. "jewel of the first water": Phrase referring to the "water," or luster or color, of a jewel; a "jewel of the first water" is something of the highest order.

2. oryide: A drunk or alcoholic; perhaps from Cockney slang.

HOBOES THAT PASS IN THE NIGHT

1. monica: moniker or nickname.

2. October 15, 1894: London erred; "B.W. 9-15-94" stands for September 15, 1894.

3. "Faro . . . craps": Faro is a card game popular in the nineteenth-century West; craps is a dice game.

4. leeward: Side with the wind, rather than against it; the direction that the wind is blowing.

5. pedro: Card game popular in the late nineteenth-century West.

6. "carried the banner": "Carrying the banner" is hobo slang for walking the streets all night without money for shelter; walking helps in avoiding vagrancy arrest.

ROAD-KIDS AND GAY-CATS

1. "Paradise Lost": Book-length poem by John Milton (1608–1674) telling the story of Creation and the Fall of humanity; in the poem, Lucifer expresses pride in his refusal to submit to God's will.

2. halyards: Lines used to raise and lower a sail.

3. "I belayed and ran aft to the tiller": London stopped and quickly ran to the rear of the boat to control the rudder.

4. passear: Portuguese for "wander" or "travel."

TWO THOUSAND STIFFS

1. gunwales: Top of a boat's sides; something "loaded to the gunwales" is completely full.

2. C.B. & Q.: Chicago, Burlington & Quincy Railroad.

3. Cannon-ball: Popular nickname for the Wabash Railroad that ran passenger trains to Chicago; from the folk song "Wabash Cannonball."

4. C. & A.: Chicago and Alton Railroad.

5. Masson City: Mason City, Iowa.

6. "Dr. Jordan's test of truth": David Starr Jordan (1851–1931), American naturalist, educator, and first president of Stanford University.

BULLS

1. gamins: street children.

2. Prisoner-of-Chillon: "The Prisoner of Chillon" (1816) is a poem by George Gordon, Lord Byron (1788–1824), about a prisoner kept in a dungeon for many years.

3. "making passes and not dragging down": A "pass" bet in craps gambles that a certain number, the "point," will be rolled before a seven; "dragging down" means collecting the pot. In the game London describes, the tension grew because the bet had not yet won or lost.

About the Editor

Todd DePastino is the author of *Citizen Hobo: How a Century of Homelessness Shaped America* (University of Chicago Press, 2003) and a forthcoming biography of cartoonist and author Bill Mauldin (W. W. Norton). He is an independent historian who teaches history at Waynesburg College and Penn State Beaver. He lives and works in Pittsburgh, Pennsylvania.